SPANKING

The Erotic Guide to Relationship Discipline

Marisa Rudder

Marisa Rudder

Author of Love & Obey, Real Men Worship Women and Oral Sex for Women

Available on Amazon Books.

Please contact: Marisa Rudder

Email: femaleledrelationshipbook@gmail.com

Printed in the United States of America Publisher's Cataloging-in-Publication data

ISBN: 978-0-9991804-0-2

Dedication

I would like to dedicate this book to all the strong, brave ladies who have joined or about to join the Love & Obey movement and live a female led lifestyle and the supportive gentlemen who recognized the natural superiority of females. It is also my desire that women and men experience the joy, happiness and passion from exploring all aspects of a loving Female Led Relationship (FLR) and understanding all the benefits of a loving female authority. If you have not already, please join us on social media.

You can find out more at our website:
www.loveandobey.com

Or follow me on social media:

FACEBOOK

https://www.facebook.com/femaleledrelationships

TWITTER

https://twitter.com/loveandobeybook

INSTAGRAM

https://www.instagram.com/femaleledrelationships

WARNING

This book contains adult sexual content. It should not be read by anyone under the age of 18 years. In addition to sexually explicit and descriptive content, this book contains controversial sexual discussions about spanking, discipline and Female Led Relationships.

Introduction

Why is the fantasy of spanking so exciting? Men and women have both admitted to having fantasies of being tied up and whipped. More couples have admitted to engaging in spanking and adding it to their sex lives. I can recall the number of times men begged me to spank them in bed. Being a strong, fully capable woman, they were excited at the thought of being under my control, and I was fully physically capable of administering a very heavy-handed spanking that could bring, even the biggest, aggressive man to tears. I could see how spanking could spice up any sex life and how it led to some very interesting and adventurous love-making. Men became obsessed and many of them began to almost need it to feel fully under their woman's control.

In a Female Led Relationship, the desire to be controlled by a strong female becomes even more important. More women are taking control in many aspects of their lives and many are leading countries, governments, corporations, cities, households and now the bedroom. My previous books *Love & Obey* and *Real Men Worship Women* are blockbuster hits and provide the essential guidance that a couple needs to build a lasting, successful relationship. Part of keeping the spark alive in all relationships is to add discipline. Relationship discipline takes spanking to a whole new level in the sex life, and a better sex life naturally means a better relationship in many cases.

Why has spanking become so popular? Our desire to engage in spanking comes out of our need for attention. The only time most children get attention is when their parents are disciplining them, and maybe as adults we crave this undivided attention. Though spanking children is not advisable and outlawed, spanking in the bedroom has skyrocketed. As the leader of the Love & Obey and Female Led Relationship movement, I have seen how spanking has particularly become popular with women spanking men. So, I will be exploring spanking as it pertains to fun displays of discipline and dominance in the relationship.

Though spanking comes out of BDSM, this book is in no way intended to instruct on the particular practices or customs of BDSM. The intention of this book is to focus on fun things the Queen can do to discipline her man in a playful respectful way if the man desires it and there is full consent. I will also touch lightly on spanking as a means of serious discipline for those couples who wish to learn more about this and, of course, how spanking can be added to as part of relationship discipline. Overall, spanking during sex is meant to add some variety and that element of fun and adventure to any relationship.

During one of the first parties I've ever attended for fetish, a massive gathering with thousands of people were moving through a maze of different rooms set up with everything to do with BDSM, bondage and torture. It was straight out of the movie *Eyes Wide Shut*. In one room, I observed an old man getting saran wrapped and strung up, hanging from the rafters. Three dominatrixes prepared themselves like a scene out of the movie *Wonder Woman* on the island of Themyscira when the female warriors were preparing for battle. Then once they were armed with their floggers, they began to flog the man while we all watched. But what I cannot stop thinking about was the smile on his face. He urged them to beat him harder and more.

They would replace their floggers for riding crops, and no matter how hard they whipped the man, he just got happier and seemed to be in a state of ecstasy. This got me thinking about the idea of spanking in the bedroom and how both the fear of what it could be, and the painful sensations wake up something primal in both men and women. Something which cannot be achieved with any other sexual act. Men who want to be dominated are intensely turned on and the women derive a great deal of satisfaction from completely controlling her man.

Think of the intense excitement you will feel when your Queen ties you up, teases you to death with role-playing, ticklers and light strokes of a whip. For some, this is a way of life. I know many couples who cannot wait to engage in some kind of dominance play and relationship discipline. Women have admitted to me the satisfaction they get when they can control their men, spank them whenever they want, and they have their men begging for more and treating them infinitely better than before.

Spanking can cause many of our deep desires for complete attention from our partners because let's face it, you need complete, undivided attention when administering and receiving a spanking. It resolves many of the disrespectful behaviors that have arisen and are accepted by society as normal, but which can lead to the unraveling and the eventual destruction of the relationship. How many times have I seen couples spending quality time together and they are on their phones or social media? Spanking in the bedroom is the one time a couple's minds do not wander, and you can't be on the phone. To partake in spanking and relationship discipline, there cannot be distractions, and this is one of the advantages to the relationship.

Within the world of dominance and submission, discipline is often eroticized and executed in a way society wouldn't otherwise condone. But many couples are waking up a dead sex life with the addition of spanking and light BDSM.

In the Female Led Relationships, more men have admitted that they enjoy and have a strong desire for their women to whip them and be aggressive. Hence, this book will deal with erotic spanking and how the Queen can administer this discipline to her man during sex. Today, more relationships are being led by women. Women are taking charge in the household and in the bedroom. Men are loving the experience of being under the spell and the dominance of women and spanking just adds to the feeling of control for the Queen. When women feel empowered, then they are at their best and men get excited when they take charge and show their power. So. it's a win-win for most.

The popularity of spanking shows no signs of slowing down.

Spanking is fast becoming the favorite bedroom pastime and at 670,000 searches a month, it shows that its popularity worldwide is only growing. A recent survey showed that 75 percent of women and 66 percent of men enjoyed erotic spanking. This book will serve as an introduction to erotic spanking, and it will provide some fun ideas on how to add spanking to your sexual routine in a safe way. It cannot be understated that safety is the key as well as consent. This must always be a pastime between consenting adults who are in a committed relationship. Added to an already healthy sex life, spanking can be a fun way to spice up the bedroom while fulfilling your fantasies.

When a couple begins a female led lifestyle, they need to discuss how they want to go about it. Are they going to agree on a list of rules first, or will they agree that the female leader will train the man as she sees fit? Some couples prefer the former while others prefer the latter. Each individual couple must figure out what works for them. In my first book, *Love & Obey*, I used positive reinforcement behavioral training to encourage good behavior, and I do not endorse the use of non-consensual, physical punishment. Today, I still only endorse safe physical punishment, which is consensual and not harmful in any lasting or serious way. A couple must always fully agree before engaging in this practice and both should be adults.

I have come to see why spanking, paddling, whipping and caning is important and is such a popular and erotic form of training men, especially in a Female Led Relationship. Obedience must be demanded by the Queen, if she wishes to rule over each man. A Female Led Relationship may start out as a male sexual fantasy, but it must evolve into a real lifestyle in which the woman really leads, and the man really obeys, or it simply will not work. Spanking and relationship discipline has the ability to be a fun pastime to your sexual routine, or it has the power to transform the relationship and increase intimacy and respect.

Marisa Rudder

Table of Contents

CHAPTER **1**

What is Spanking?

S panking has become one of the most popular activities in the bedroom, and it is fast becoming a favorite pastime for many couples. Spanking is described as a common form of corporal punishment, involving the act of striking the butt or some other area of another person, to cause physical pain. More severe forms of spanking, such as switching, paddling, belting, caning, whipping and birching, involve the use of an object instead of a hand. Spanking began in slavery and as part of the punishment of children. There has been an outcry against spanking children today as researchers raise questions about the long-term psychological effects on people, so it is losing popularity with parents and is occurring much less than it used to. But spanking is witnessing a rise in the bedroom, which is fast becoming one of the most popular additions to many couples' sex life.

For years, spanking was depicted in movies when a man felt the need to control a woman he thought was out of control. There are film scenes where men are seen grabbing his woman, throwing her over his leg and slapping her behind. Old episodes of *I Love Lucy* to the 2004 *Along Came Polly* depict this behavior, and even Justin Timberlake promised in his 2006 single "SexyBack," by singing "I'll let you whip me if I misbehave." Rihanna also sings about whips and chains in "S&M," and in the Netflix series *Weeds,* Nancy Botwin gets a good spanking from Esteban, the head of the cartel.

Today, particularly in the bedroom, the tides are turning, and men are being spanked by the women who they now serve as their Queen. There is growing interest in spanking as more and more couples are engaging in it. Sex expert Sienna Sinclaire says, "Erotic spanking is all about spanking someone for sexual pleasure for both parties." The person being spanked enjoys it and the person doing the spanking is also getting enjoyment. Spanking has become so popular that now there are thousands of products available on Amazon to ensure you can create the perfect spanking experience. But is spanking during sex a new concept? Apparently not.

Erotic spanking became extremely popular during the Renaissance where it was practiced openly in French courts. It also grew in popularity in Victorian England. More recently, erotic spanking gained international appeal in the 1940s in Bizarre magazine, which published illustrated fetish stories and articles. In the 1970s, spanking groups sprang up around the United States, many of which are still active today, such as Shadow Lane, Crimson Moon and Paddles Club NYC, with the most famous retreats organized by spanking, BDSM and fetish film director Carter Stevens. But some of the really early depictions of spanking can be seen in ancient Egyptian and Italian art.

Getting smacked on the butt was a real turn on for centuries, and many couples spank each other and give a little tap on the butt just for fun. You can see spanking or taps on the butt in sports as a gesture of support by a teammate. And, of course, there is no end to spanking references in movies like *Fifty Shades of Grey* in which it was definitely what Christian

Grey enjoyed the most in his encounters with Anastasia Steele. Spanking was thrust into the mainstream after this film. Join any dominatrix group or watch any dominatrix videos and you'll realize spanking is one of the most requested activities by men. There is simply a great desire for men to experience being tied up or put over their mistress's knee to be spanked for bad behavior or fun.

Today, in Female Led Relationships, many men enjoy being spanked by their Queen, and many have introduced it as an acceptable weekly—even daily—occurrence. Learning proper technique and ways to introduce it into the sex life is key. I will be discussing all aspects of erotic spanking, including the history, proper techniques, tools, and much more. The goal of this book is to help men and women engage in fun, healthy, safe, and consensual spanking as part of their sex routine. I will also add some information on the serious practice of relationship discipline, and I will touch lightly on BDSM.

It is my wish that all couples use this as a way to build more intimacy and spice up your sex life. A healthy, fun sex life can dramatically change your relationship for the better. Spanking is a pivotal part of the Female Led Relationship where the woman administers the spanking both for fun times as well as discipline. Being the leader of the Love and Obey movement, which promotes a healthy and safe female led lifestyle, spanking with consent from both the Queen and her man fits perfectly into the female led world. Women are already in charge and more than capable of giving a great spanking session. Spanking has the power to transform a relationship from dull, boring, monotonous and failing to exciting, intimate and rewarding. Happy safe spanking.

Marisa Rudder

CHAPTER 2

Why is Spanking Such a Turn on?

So why is spanking growing and why is it such a turn on? Men have been known to crave fantasies of being dominated and women love powerful men. According to a study by a new paper published in the journal *Social Psychological and Personality Science* by Joris Lammers and Roland Imhoff, social power reduces inhibition. In other words, powerful, even wealthy, men are aroused by being dominated by women in bed. In one of the earliest episodes of the show *Game of Thrones*, Khaleesi after taking it from her husband played by Jason Momoa, she is instructed to dominate him. Once she does this, she is treated like a Queen and a Goddess. But another study claims that power frees people from their inhibitions, and thereby increases sadomasochistic thoughts in everyone, masochistic tendencies in men who are being hurt or tortured and sadistic thoughts in women. So, this is the reason why men crave torture and are turned on when aggressive women do this particularly during sex.

The findings of the study showed that power increases the arousal to sadomasochism. Furthermore, the effect of power on arousal by sadistic thoughts is stronger among women than men, while the effect of power on arousal by masochistic thoughts is stronger among men than women. Masochistic is defined as deriving sexual gratification from one's own pain or humiliation. As was uncovered, men crave physical torture from dominant women, and this coincides with my findings as well. Men simply love the pain felt when a powerful woman smacks them on the behind, and the powerful woman is turned on by doing the act. A 2013 study found that both dominant and submissive practitioners of BDSM were less neurotic, more extroverted, more open to new experiences, more conscientious, and less sensitive to rejection. They also had higher subjective well-being compared to the control group. This could mean two things: People with these traits are attracted to kinky sex, or kinky sex can help you grow and gain confidence.

I always think of the scene from *The Wolf of Wall Street* where Jordan Belfort is so taken with his dominatrix Venice that he was caught calling out her name in his sleep. In the scene, Venice's preferred punishment is to pour candle wax on his butt while whipping him, and he enjoys it so much that he is dreaming about it. But Mr. Belfort, a powerful head of an investment firm, craved this activity despite having access to thousands of women from all walks of life in various sexual escapades yet this is the one he dreams about.

There are many reasons as to why erotic spanking is exciting. First, there's the physical sensation. If done properly, spanking stimulates a person's genitals indirectly and creates a subtle sensation that is, no doubt, pleasurable. On the other hand, there's the psychological aspect of it. Erotic spanking can also have a lot to do with role-play and pretend-punishment that flares up one's imagination and makes the sexual experience much more intense.

BDSM, which stands for bondage and discipline, dominance and submission, and sadism and masochism, and spanking can allow people to begin experiencing this practice in a fun way. Spanking comes out of BDSM. Discipline in BDSM is the practice in which the dominant sets rules that the submissive is expected to obey. When rules of expected behaviors are broken, punishment is often used as a means of disciplining. In BDSM , rules can be made so that a submissive or sub knows how they should behave so that the dominant is not displeased.

In Female Led Relationships, this translates into men behaving properly according to the rules of the Queen. Rules can also be for reminding subs of their inferior status, or for training a novice sub. In BDSM, when such rules are broken, punishment is often used as a means of discipline. Punishment itself can be physical such as caning, or psychological such as public humiliation or a combination of both- through bondage and spanking. So, spanking during sex extends from this practice of BDSM and discipline, which becomes a fun way for the Queen to exert her dominance over her man for both of their enjoyment.

What turns on one person about spanking is personal. Shelby Devlin, a sex and intimacy coach, says that the person getting spanked may love the feeling of powerlessness, while another person might only be about the physical sensation. So, when you first decide you want to explore spanking, she may suggest to take time out for self-reflection. What is it about spanking that turns you and your partner on? Analyze it and discuss it.

Dawn Michael, a certified sexuality counselor and marriage and family therapist with a Ph.D. in human sexuality, says that being submissive or dominant with your partner can be a sexy role-play that spanking easily falls under. She says that "spanking can be a turn on for both a man and a woman who enjoy being submissive to their partner, working it into a role of submission to their Dom for a man or their master for a woman."

Men have always loved aggressive woman and spanking in sex offers the opportunity for women to take control and spice things up during sex. Imagine an entire foreplay session in which she ties you up, blindfolds you, and throws you down on the bed, and runs her flogger or horse whip all the way up from your toes to your head, then gives you a few slaps. Afterward, she gets on top and rides you to orgasm. Who can resist?

Almost everyone has some secret desire, fantasy, or fetish that turns them on in the bedroom or elsewhere. Some choose to keep their fantasies to themselves and think about them when they're alone. They consider this part of their sexuality not necessary to share. However, others have a strong urge to share their fantasy or fetish, desiring to act it out with partners. Feelings of guilt, shame, and confusion about our fantasies and what turns us on are common in our society. What is often difficult for people to understand is that sexual awakening happens when we are children. Although childhood sexuality is a natural part of development, it is often ignored in our culture, shunned, or brushed under the rug as wrong. The child is made to feel ashamed or guilty for having sexual thoughts and desires. No explanations are given, and nothing is talked about.

CHAPTER 3

What is the History of Spanking?

T he history of spanking dates back to 490 BC. In Italy, the Whipping Tomb paintings were discovered and showed a scene of two men getting pleasure while flogging a woman in a sexual manner. The scene is reminiscent of Dionysus as the god of the grape-harvest, winemaking and wine, of fertility in Greek mythology. He is considered "the liberator" and his wine, music and ecstatic dance frees his followers from self-conscious fear and concern and subverts the oppressive restraints of the powerful. Those who partake his mysteries are believed to become possessed and empowered by the god himself.

The Etruscan burial site was called the Tomba della Fustigazione or "Tomb of Flogging" after its depictions of eroticized flagellation. These may have been related to the pre-Roman holiday of Lupercalia, the original pagan Valentine's Day, which features light public spankings and whippings instead of, or in addition to, the traditional kisses and candy of our modern Valentine's day. In Medieval times, with overt pagan pleasures denied, Catholic saints and penitents indulged in auto-flagellation to reach states of mystical consciousness that bordered on the erotic.

And it's not just Italians. For thousands of years, Taoist Chinese have engaged in a similar ritual of spanking and whipping during the Spring Festivals of their Lunar New Year, the stated purpose of which is to get rid of "bad luck." The Indian Kama Sutra contains multiple descriptions of how to "strike" your partner's buttocks, as well as other body parts, during sex. Tibetan monks have long whipped each other for medicinal and spiritual purposes. In Latvia, Sweden, Hungary, Slovakia, Poland and Czech Republic, it is customary for the young men to awaken the young ladies on Palm Sunday, Good Friday, Shrove Tuesday or Easter Monday by dousing them with water and spanking them on the butt and legs with colorful Easter whips in a playfully aggressive way.

Later on, Sadism is named after Marquis de Sade (1740-1814), a French nobleman and soldier, who spent many years in prisons and asylums, much of it for sexual behavior that was considered abhorrent. He also wrote novels describing scenes of sexual cruelty. Next was Freud, and though he is not considered the authority on sex and sexuality, it would be foolish to deny the impact he had on society. Although Freud's theories and therapy were rooted in misogyny and opinion, he did something no other psychological professional in the Western world had done before him: He openly talked about sex and sexual identity development. This laid the groundwork for our current sexual world and profession, one in which we can now talk about sex and have space to assist clients working through sexuality-related concerns.

Elizabeth Ehrmann wrote of Freud's three forms of masochism in her study titled, "The Economic Problem of Masochism." In this study, Freud distinguished three forms of masochism: erotogenic, feminine and moral. Freud regarded the first two forms of masochism as secondary to sadism, and a turning inward of this upon the self because you enjoy having pain inflicted upon yourself. The third kind, moral masochism, is different because it is not obviously erotic, not physical and has no special relations to significant persons. According to Freud, it is the suffering or self-injury itself that matters, no matter who inflicts it, whether it is a person or fate.

The moral form of masochism plays an extensive part in social life because it is an abusive internal monologue, and in analysis, it represents perhaps the most difficult problem to solve. Freud proposed the concept of "moral masochism," in which the practice was recast as the unconscious desire for punishment borne of guilt. So, from here, it was not considered related to sexuality but in a category all on its own. Ehermann's also wrote in the article "Sadomasochism According to Freud's Psychosexual Stages of Development Theory" that according to Freud, the combination of children being sexual, and perhaps the repeated act of spanking, whipping, or beating, is believed to lead to a life of sadomasochism. If Freud's theory is correct, children who have experienced spankings or whippings will tend to be or would desire to be a sadomasochist, hence an interest in pain and spanking in adulthood. There is no doubt that spanking wakes up something inside us, particularly those who are very aroused and excited by it.

Through Freud's psychosexual stages of development theory, a better understanding of the sexual deviation, "sadomasochism" will ideally be reached. The six psychosexual stages of development are oral, anal, phallic, latent, and genital. Through each of these different stages, Freud believed that sexual outcomes originate. In addition, Freud's Oedipus complex offers some clues to the desire for spanking. The Oedipus complex explains the emotions and ideas that the mind keeps in the unconscious, via dynamic repression, that concentrates upon a child's desire to have sexual relations with the parent of the opposite sex (i.e., males attracted to their mothers, and females attracted to their fathers).

The Oedipus complex also suggests that boys will be fearful of their fathers, and this is resolved through identification where they copy the behavior of their fathers. The same occurs with the girl and their mothers. Therefore, it is this identification which leads to boys and girls—of parents who are aggressive and administer punishment, like spanking—to also have a similar desire and exhibit similar behavior. If a boy grew up with his father being dominated by a strong mother, then he will crave this role in his own partner. Today, many men and women are raised in single parent households where the mother takes control and must be the strong dominant parent, which explains why there is an increased number of men craving Female Led Relationships and more women who crave to lead the relationship. It also explains the desire of men to be dominated in bed by their women.

We often think that spanking is masochism, but the psychologist Roy Baumeister noted that the nonsexual behaviors often characterized as "masochistic" differ qualitatively from sexual masochism in that it tends to be self-destructive and self-defeating. Sexual masochism, on the other hand, is neither destructive nor self-defeating. Sexual masochists neither seek nor regularly experience injury. Rather, they engage in carefully negotiated rituals of humiliation and the infliction of pain often through spanking and discipline. Data suggest that sexual masochists as a group are generally normal in all other aspects of their lives and psychologically healthy.

In a recent survey of over 1,500 adults, more than one-third of women and more than one-quarter of men reported having fantasized about being spanked or whipped. There are many additional theories for masochism, which includes any behavior that runs counter to our day-to-day habits will be deemed arousing. In other words, if you spend your days being powerful and in control, the feeling of powerlessness and the loss of control will be arousing.

In terms of torture, Stanley Milgram was one of the first people to study it in the Milgram experiment on obedience to authority figures, which was a series of social psychology experiments conducted by Yale University. The study measured the willingness of men to respond to an authority figure to conduct acts on others against their conscience. The results indicated that a high proportion of men were willing to do this. It suggests that under the right circumstances, and with the appropriate encouragement and setting, men will respond to an authority figure and be completely obedient— as in the case of the woman who is their Queen.

It is my belief that based on these theories, and the fact that the US divorce rate is at 60 percent, 83 percent of single parent households are headed by the mother. Currently, one in four kids under the age of 18 are raised without a father, or about 16.4 million children. So, a significant number of people are raised in single parent homes where the mother is dominant. According to Freud's theory, men will have the desire for their mothers who generally now have to be strong independent women and will primarily do the disciplining, hence the man's desire for discipline from a strong woman in a Female Led Relationship.

In Freud's theory of identification, women will want to be like their mothers, hence they will naturally take charge and be assertive in their intent to do the disciplining. Merge these two and you get a very strong sexual desire for men to seek out strong women in a Female Led Relationship and their desire to engage in aggression, like being spanked by a partner capable of doing the spanking. It is my belief that there will be a growing trend for erotic spanking.

Research shows that men are responsible for over 90 percent of serious violent crimes, such as assaults, homicides, and violent robberies. Why is there such a large gender gap and is it likely to persist? One might imagine that lower violent crime rates for women reflects a generally lower level of aggression. Yet marriage researchers observe the opposite pattern. Women are more likely to pick fights with their husbands, are quicker to escalate verbal aggression, and are likely to use physical aggression than men. Modern women are behaving much more like men when it comes to risk-taking and aggression. One sign of this phenomenon is greater participation in contact sports and dangerous competitions, such as horse racing or car racing. According to Anthropologist Elizabeth Cashdan, societies where women compete more amongst each other, whether in occupations, or over spouses, their levels of stress hormones and testosterone increase. These women enjoy taking charge, and they admit to having no problem being aggressive with men.

In the 17th century, two German authors made their name in spanking research: the German physician Johann Heinrich Meibom, who wrote a best-selling treatise on the use of flogging as a medical and sexual stimulant, and German medical botanist and poet Kristian Frantz Paullini, whose *Flagellum Salutis* praised flagellation for its curative use in treating diseases as diverse as melancholia, paralysis, toothache, sleepwalking, deafness, and nymphomania, as well as for pleasure and sexual arousal. So, spanking has been around for centuries, and today it is alive and well and enjoyed by many couples as part of their sexual life.

CHAPTER 4

Spanking & BDSM

S panking falls under the umbrella of BDSM. As noted earlier in this book, BDSM is the acronym for bondage, discipline, submission, masochism, and it's a practice that's ancient. According to research, there's evidence of BDSM sex practices in ancient Greek art, and the Kama Sutra, which was written in 300 AD, publicized erotic spanking as a way to add a little something extra to people's sex lives. Although, the number of participants will remain a mystery.

Unfortunately, BDSM has been misunderstood. Italian researchers recently surveyed the sexuality of 266 Italian men and women who enjoy bondage, discipline, and sadomasochism (BDSM). The study population ranged in age from 18 to 74 with an average of 41. The researchers also surveyed 200 demographically similar men and women not involved in BDSM. The two groups reported similar feelings about their sexuality, but the BDSM players reported less sexual distress and greater erotic satisfaction. The researchers said they hoped their study would reduce the stigma associated with it.

BDSM has emerged from the underground and is now out in the open. It involves a power exchange and has the potential to make relationships more sexually fulfilling, but just like all relationships, it's a matter of communicating wants and desires. And just like in other bad relationships, abuse and manipulation can happen, but that is a matter of individual personalities and relationships, not a characteristic of BDSM as a whole. Psychologist Kasi Alexander says, "It's important to make a distinction between mental conditions and different sexual preferences and alternative lifestyles. The most important aspect of the mental disorder consideration is the difference between true sadism and kinky sadism." A vast majority of 'sadists' in the BDSM community derive no pleasure from inflicting pain unless the recipient is enjoying the experience, whereas a true sadist is not concerned with the other person's benefit.

People are not just talking about it more openly than they did in the past, but they're also practicing BDSM in their own sex lives. According to OkCupid's 2015 Hangover report, 58 percent of users have a desire to participate in bondage. But how many actually do? *Psychology Today* explores a variety of questions such as: What kinds of personality types engage in BDSM? Do people who engage in BDSM come from abusive families? Why would someone want to engage in BDSM play? Is BDSM abuse? Are BDSM relationships cold, distant, controlling, or abusive? What kind of feelings do people who engage in BDSM experience before, during, and after intense sensation play?

The magazine also conducted a study involving more than 200 participants who engage in BDSM. Information was obtained from respondents via an online survey, consisting of roughly twelve qualitative questions about the individual's motivations and experiences engaging in BDSM, as well as three psychological instruments: the Experiences in Close

Relationships Scale-Short Form (ECR-S), which measures attachment style; the Adverse Childhood Experiences Scale (ACE), which measures level of childhood trauma; and the Big Five Inventory (BFI), which measures personality traits.

The findings were as follows: No significant difference between people who engage in BDSM and those who don't in traumatic childhood experiences, such as feeling neglected, having divorced or separated parents, witnessing the abuse of a parent, or living with substance or alcohol abusers. People who engage in BDSM had significantly higher scores on the BFI openness to new experiences. Last, no significant difference between people who engage in BDSM and people who don't in anxious or avoidant attachment styles. This means that BDSM participants are not more likely than others to be uncomfortable with closeness in relationships or are they more likely to be the needy stalker type.

To summarize, those who practice BDSM do not have more pathological personality traits or insecure attachment styles, or substantially more adverse childhood experiences; neither are most of them experiencing negative feelings nor being driven by harmful motivations in their engagement of intense sensation play.

While the extent people are exploring the realms of BDSM will vary from couple to couple, even some of the "vanilla" sex people have probably picked up a blindfold and at least considered integrating it into their sex lives. In 2015, Indiana University researchers surveyed a representative sample of 2,021 American adults. Many said they had tried some elements of BDSM as revealed in the following statistics: 30 percent spanking, 22 percent dominant/submissive role-playing, 20 percent restraint, and 13 percent flogging.

In 2017, Belgian scientists surveyed 1,027 Belgian adults in which forty-seven percent admitted to experimenting with

BDSM. Thirteen percent said they experimented that way regularly. Eight percent said they felt committed to BDSM sexuality.

BDSM is all about discipline in which the goal is to teach the sub that they have made a mistake for the purpose of learning self-restraint and becoming a better sub in the future. The punishment is typically related to the mistake and is proportionate to the severity and frequency of the mistake. In BDSM there are two things that must not be confused—the disciplining of the sub and sadomasochism (S&M), involves giving pain or torture to a "sub" for sexual enjoyment.

Contrarily, punishments for disciplining are in response to violations of predetermined rules or for otherwise displeasing the dominant. Punishment is considered necessary, as without it, a sub may repeat mistakes and thus not improve in their role. So, spanking during sex would be considered a lighter version of both branches of BDSM, but it should not be considered a pure version as there is a serious art and practice of BDSM to be followed. But since erotic spanking has emerged from BDSM, it is fun to explore. The man is the sub and the woman is the Queen and dominant.

In spanking role-play, the Queen must administer a spanking for her man's disobedience. A fun way to do this is if you disrespect your Queen in any way, such as making fun of her, failing to listen to her or abide to her rules, , then she can command you to stand up, pull down your pants, and give you a sweet spanking before leading to sex. Some couples enjoy just giving the spanking as daily discipline, others prefer to begin with the spanking, which can lead to being so turned on you must have hot passionate sex after this.

Some Commonly Used Terms in BDSM:

Aftercare: Aftercare is post-play etiquette in which all parties check in on one another to ensure the scene was enjoyable, tend to any bruises as well as emotional needs, and communicate how all parties feel.

BDSM: Stands for Bondage, Discipline, Sadism, and Masochism, and is an umbrella term for any kinky play that involves a consensual power exchange.

Bondage: Bondage is when one partner (typically the submissive) is tied up by the dominant partner. Bondage is frequently part of impact play, because tying up the submissive, who then consensually can't move, adds to the thrill of the scene.

Dom Drop and Sub Drop: During a BDSM scene, endorphins and adrenaline run high for all partners. As a result, like a crash from a drug, both the submissive and dominant partner may experience a comedown immediately after or even a few days later. All parties involved have a responsibility to tend to their partner during their drop.

D/S: Refers to dominance and submission. Typically, one partner takes on the dominant, or top role. In impact play, this is the person inflicting the spanks or other forms of play. The submissive is the bottom, or the person receiving the impact on their body.

Edge play: Edge play refers to BDSM activities that push the limit of what is considered safe, sane, and consensual. This often refers to activities involving bodily fluids and blood. Single-tail whips are considered a form of edge play as they can draw blood and inflict harm if not used correctly.

Hard Limits: Your hard limits are activities that are absolutely off-limits and should be communicated to your partner prior to play.

Kink: A kink refers to any sexual interest that is outside the heterosexual vanilla norm.

Pain Slut: Pain sluts are people who enjoy erotic pain.

Play: Play is a word used within the kink community to refer to any erotic activity, from penetrative intercourse to impact play.

RACK: Stands for Risk-Aware Consensual Kink and is the guideline all kinky play should follow. It means all parties understand the risks they are taking and consent.

Safe word: A safe word is a word agreed upon by all parties that indicates it's time to immediately stop the play. A safe word is used instead of "stop" or "no," as some people enjoy scenes in which they consensually "fight back."

SCC: Stands for Safe, Sane, and Consensual. It is another acronym for safety guidelines, although RACK is more commonly used today because what is considered safe and sane varies from person to person.

Scene: A scene refers to the time in which the agreed upon kinky play occurs.

Soft Limits: Soft limits are things that you are curious about but hesitant to try. Perhaps in the future you'll want to try them, but as of now, it's a no. Your limits may change with time.

Corporal punishment is a form of physical punishment that involves the deliberate infliction of pain as retribution for an offense, or for the purpose of disciplining or reforming a wrongdoer, or to deter attitudes or behavior deemed unacceptable. The term usually refers to methodically striking the offender with an implement, whether in judicial, domestic, or educational settings.

Different parts of the anatomy may be targeted, such as the buttocks—whether clothed or bare—have often been targeted for punishment, particularly in Europe and the English-speaking world.

The advantage is that these fleshy body parts are robust and can be chastised accurately, without endangering any bodily functions, and they also heal well and relatively quickly. In some cultures, punishment applied to the buttocks entails a degree of humiliation, which may or may not be intended as part of the punishment. Hitting the back of the thighs and calves is at least as painful if not more so, but this can cause more damage in terms of scars and bruising. The upper back and the shoulders have historically been a target for whipping (e.g., in the UK with the cat-o'-nine-tails in the Royal Navy and in some pre-1948 judicial punishments), and today generally in the Middle East and the Islamic world. The soles of the feet are extremely sensitive and flogging them as has sometimes been done in the Middle East.

Flagellation also falls under the umbrella of BDSM, and this is the act of spanking. It involves flogging, whipping, or lashing is the act of beating the human body with special implements such as whips, lashes, rods, switches, and the cat o' nine tails. Typically, flogging is imposed on an unwilling subject as a punishment; however, it can also be given to willingly, or performed on oneself, in religious or sadomasochistic contexts. Usually, it is the butt or back that is struck but for a moderated subform of flagellation, described as bastinado, the soles of a person's bare feet are used as a target for beating. In some circumstances, the word "flogging" is used loosely to include any sort of corporal punishment, including birching and caning.

The Flagellation, in a Christian context, refers to an episode in the Passion of Christ prior to Jesus's crucifixion. The practice of mortification of the flesh for religious purposes has been utilized by members of various Christian denominations since the time of the Great Schism in 1054. Nowadays, the instrument of penance is called a discipline, a cattail whip usually made of knotted cords, which is flung over the shoulders repeatedly during private prayer. In the 13th century, a group of Roman Catholics, known as the Flagellants, took self-mortification to extremes. These people would travel to towns and publicly beat and whip each other while preaching repentance. The nature of these demonstrations being quite morbid and disorderly, they were during periods of time suppressed by the authorities. They continued to reemerge at different times up until the 16th century. Flagellation was also practiced during the Black Plague as a means to purify oneself of sin and thus prevent contracting the disease. Pope Clement VI is known to have allowed the act for this purpose in 1348.

Martin Luther, the Protestant Reformer, regularly practiced self-flagellation as a means of mortification of the flesh. So BDSM, flagellation and spanking are all closely related, but spanking in sex is not BDSM. And BDSM is not necessarily practiced in Female Led Relationships. In *Love & Obey*, BDSM is not part of a Female Led Relationship, but it is the decision of the couple to decide if they want to add spanking to their relationship. Although spanking is done in BDSM, there are specific rules and practices that are reserved for the practice of BDSM.

CHAPTER 5

Why Do Female Led Women Love to Spank Men?

Women in Female Led Relationships love to give a good spanking to their men. Here's why: In spanking, there is a power exchange, and in a Female Led Relationship, the Queen is in charge. She has the power and the opportunity to exert her power on her man during sex with a little spanking. This can be a great turn-on for both men and women. Also, let's face it—dominance is sexy. Dominance during sex intensifies sexual drive, and powerful women drive men crazy. A woman in a position of power is the desire of every man, particularly to the man who has dedicated his life to serving.

Men are already submissive in a Female Led Relationship, so they have already agreed to their Queen having free reign over them. During sex, heightened levels of sexual pleasure begin once the woman assumes this role of dominance and even suggests spanking. Asserting your authority as a woman during sex portrays to the man that she knows what she wants and is going to have it. This makes her man eager to please and submit. It adds an element of adventure and fear, which can be extremely arousing.

It is normal for sex in long-term relationships to get monotonous and repetitive, so spanking shakes things up and allows the Queen to have the control, which is her deepest desire. I feel that spanking appeals to the deepest of desires of a female led woman, which is to have complete power over her man. Just as children get tired of their old toys, adults also get bored and tired of carrying out the same, repetitive sexual routine and styles without the introduction of something new or adventurous. Spanking adds an extra spice by bringing diversification in a regular sexual ritual. Spanking can make things very intimate as the Queen is in total control and the man is vulnerable in assuming positions for the Queen to spank him. Spanking brings about freshly ignited feelings that come with trying a different experience from the norm. This creates intimacy and transports you both to a whole new world and bonding you both in ways you never expected. Agreeing to introduce spanking to your sexual life is an intimate moment built. Carrying out the act together amplifies the bonding.

Many men have testified to feeling really good when they get a good spanking from their Queen. A certain stimulus is ignited when a man gets spanked because this triggers the dopamine receptors into action, bringing about sexual pleasure, which is an exciting time for both partners. It is important to not engage in kink shaming, which literally means the shaming of another person for their sexual fantasies, may happen occasionally. Even the most compatible partners can have wildly different sexual preferences. In any sexual relationship, you're bound to be turned on by different things. That's why it's best to be kind about it when your partner tells you something they want to try in bed, even if it's not for you. Sexual fantasies are best shared as part of "dirty talk" during sex. Others may feel more comfortable bringing up the topic during more neutral times when sex isn't actually on the table.

A psychologist and certified sex therapist advised the following: Create a safe space in which you're not in overwhelmed work mode, face each other, and have eye contact. Let them know that this might be hard for you or you've been waiting for the right moment. It's also usually easier to share something with others once you've become okay with it yourself, so if this is a kink you carry unneeded shame over, it might be good to work through that shame with a sex therapist or in your own individual time before discussing with a partner. Additionally, it's important to remember that as long as your fantasy is between two consenting adults, it's likely to be completely normal.

A female led lifestyle involves setting up some rules for a man's behavior that his Queen can monitor. If he breaks a rule, then he knows that he must be disciplined for doing so. This discipline teaches men to behave in a more submissive, obedient, and loving way. Some couples set up rules together, while others rely on the Queen alone to create them. Some rules may be suggested by the man since he wants to work on some negative aspect of his own behavior or attitudes that he believes is holding him back from becoming a more submissive and loving man.

Some couples write down the rules while others are quite happy to keep them on a purely verbal basis of agreement. Some men may have a tendency to debate the Queen's rules when they are called out for breaking them. This is not considered good behavior and can be disrespectful to the Queen. The most important point is consistency. If you both as a couple decide that light spanking be used when the man misbehaves, then the Queen must follow through with the spanking, and the man must obey.

Inconsistent rules are not normally a huge problem in female led households. The Queen cannot be unreasonable, but if it is agreed on, then both must follow through.

Many couples find it fairly simple and straightforward to agree on a consistent set of rules for his behavior. These rules may change and develop over time. They may be added or subtracted, as needed and common sense dictates. A Queen must create consistent consequences for his man's unruly behavior. This simply means that a Queen may spank a man briefly for a minor offense, but she may whip a man to tears for a more serious offense, ensuring that he is sobbing repentantly by the end of his punishment.

The amount and severity of the actual spanking may vary because the Queen may need to adjust these based on the man's attitude, but the relative outcomes must be consistent. Light spanking for a very minor offense, and heavy paddling with tears for a more serious offense. The consequence of a man's different types of bad behavior must be consistent, even if they are not identical. Delivering consistent consequences for male bad behavior is about maintaining the relative differences between offenses, so that it is always clear to the reason for the punishment according to the seriousness of his bad behavior. He should know that if he gets a light spanking for an insignificant offense, he will get a severe whipping for a serious offense.

CHAPTER **6**

Why Men Love Strong Women and Discipline

Today, women are now freer to assert their dominance over men and men cannot resist a strong woman. Furthermore, many men welcome discipline from their Queens. Strong women are perceived as exciting and anything can happen. Bad girls are the ones who will throw a man down, tie him up, strip off his pants and tease him until he can't stand it anymore. Who can resist giving up all of the power to a sexy, dominant woman who is fully capable of taking charge? Also, an unstable hierarchy can cause men considerable anxiety. However, an established chain of command, such as those practiced by the military and many workplaces, reduces testosterone and curbs male aggression. When a man knows his Queen is in charge and agrees, he will be calmer and easier to deal with.

In *Psychology Today,* after looking into the mating preferences of more than 5,000 men and women by way of survey, researcher and biological anthropologist Helen Fisher, Ph.D., writes that men desire smart, strong, successful women. Her article showed that 87 percent of men said they would date a woman who was more intellectual than they were, who was better educated, and who made considerably more money than they did, while 86 percent said they were in search of a woman who was confident and self-assured.

Strong women go after the things they want in life. They don't sit by and just wait for love to fall into their lap. They're not afraid to flirt and show a true interest but they also define what they want in a relationship. They let a man know right away if they're looking for a simple hookup or if they're after a real relationship, and they don't stick around if a guy wants something different. Men don't have to guess with strong women, and they can sit back and let her make the first move and take control. This is the opposite of most other areas of life in which they must compete. With a woman in charge, they are free to allow her to lead and make decisions. This also makes the woman happier and a happier woman is a much sexier woman.

Here are some tips and tricks to heat up any sex life:

1. Be the Boss in Bed Tonight

An assertive, sexy woman knows how to exploit the power she has over a man. Force your man to lie down on the bed, then use handcuffs, scarves, or a necktie to tether your hands together so that he can't touch you. Next, pull out the paddles and slowly move it along the body. Slowly kiss your way down his torso, and just as you get to his pelvis, move back up to his ears and neck. Then, turn him around and give him a couple of whacks. As you tease him and he strains to touch you, ask him to tell you why he wants you so bad. Depending on his response, you can give him a few more smacks.

2. Put on a Naughty Costume

To really turn up the heat, put on a hot costume, such as a sexy police officer or sexy sheriff, even GI Jane or sexy Rambo.

Get creative. There is a reason a dominatrix always wears their signature costume. Pleather and leather are always great ways to show you are an assertive Queen. Then give him a role. Is he the submissive slave? or the servant. Is he the pool boy or a construction worker? Maybe he's your little horsey, and you need to ride him and tame him at the same time. Let your imagination go.

3. Learn to Talk Dirty

The commanding tone like, "You will do as I say" will set the mood for spanking. Or simply "I'm going to put you over my knee." Talking dirty heightens the whole experience and men love to be ordered around by a bossy woman. Even teasing language can go over well, such as, "You like that? You like how that paddle feels going up your leg?" "How about now when I smack your butt?" "You have been a bad boy and now it's time to get your spanking". Language can be extremely seductive. Men love the sound of an aggressive, commanding woman.

4. Watch Yourselves Having Sex in a Big Mirror

Body confidence and carnal curiosity are key traits of a sex goddess, and both are on full display when you see yourselves in a mirror. It may give you a voyeuristic thrill—almost as though you're peeping into your own bedroom. It feels taboo. Let him see the restraints and whips you have in store for him. It's a thrill and a turn on for him to see you tying him up and giving him a spanking.

7. Punish the Bad Boy

Randomly put your man over your knee and get out a paddle. Pull down his pants and give him a few taps. Tie him to a table so that you are free to hit his backside. Nothing more exciting than getting physical and having him submit fully to you. Most men are thrilled when a woman wants to be aggressive with them. I feel that women can feel empowered during sex to give the spanking and feel like they are able to release pent up energy with some discipline. Men love being the bad boy, and I believe they crave their mommy to discipline them, hence the excitement of having the Queen be aggressive with them.

Given the enormous variability in activities that people find arousing, there is no one way to be sexual. Men are especially stimulated by visual imagery, and about 90 percent of young men report using pornography with some regularity, sometimes because they lack a partner or don't know how to bridge the differences in sexual appetite and interest that can occur between partners in the absence of discussion of their sexual pleasures, and sometimes for convenience. Many people engage in behaviors that were once perceived as atypical, such as dominance play and anal intercourse. Researchers know that flexibility in sexual repertoires is healthy and generally enhances relationships. They also regard a specific behavior as problematic only when it creates harm or distress for one or both partners and when the behavior is compulsive.

Today, men are exploring submission, particularly in a Female Led Relationship, and the one thing that they all discover above anything else is that male submission brings harmony to a home. There is no longer a power struggle between two people who both want to be "in charge." It is a confession of our dependence on one another and an acceptance of our natural roles—the woman as the leader, the Queen, and the man as her obedient and loyal subject.

Do you submit to your boss? If you are given instructions, do you follow them? If you don't, you would face discipline, wouldn't you?! Your Queen is simply the "boss" of your home, and you must obey her or face discipline and other forms of punishment. Many patriarchal men see submission as a form of femininity. But in fact, it is much more of a form of chivalry, like the code of the knights serving a queen. So, when a man serves his wife or girlfriend, it's not out of weakness, but out of strength. A queen may discipline a disobedient knight so that he learns real men serve their superior woman. Discipline is necessary to remind men of their role and men should embrace the loving and caring spanking, paddling, caning, and whipping discipline of their Queen.

Men in Female Led Relationships are looking for strong women. Consistency makes a man feel he has been justly disciplined when he is spanked for misbehavior or disobedience. He believes his spanking is part of a consistent and fair system of FLR rules and consequences. The FLR rules outline which behaviors are acceptable and the consequences dictate what kinds of punishment are necessary for breaking the rules. The justness of a discipline is not always the most crucial issue when it comes to female led discipline. A man will still gain great emotional and moral benefit from the occasionally unjust discipline. It will still be useful and effective in the context of a Female Led Relationship. After all, Upkeep Discipline is inherently "unjust," on the face of things, yet Upkeep Discipline is extremely effective and beneficial for any man in a Female Led Relationship.

One important reason why a man needs consistency in a Female Led Relationship is because it helps to remind him who the boss is. If he ever forgets, consistent discipline will teach him that his Queen is the boss—not him. A consistent approach to disciplining a man for masculine misbehavior is critical for maintaining his respect and love for his Queen in her role as the leader of their relationship. If a man has been well-behaved for some time, then he can easily forget his responsibilities to himself and to his Queen. Forgetting his woman is also his Queen can lead him into temptation. It can increase the likelihood of masculine misbehavior. Consistent discipline will quickly and effectively resolve this problem.

Aggression is a complex social behavior with many causes and manifestations. Over the past several decades, scholars have identified many forms of aggression. Aggression can be physical or verbal. It can be direct in nature or indirect with aim of inflicting reputational harm (e.g., spreading rumors about a co-worker behind their back). Aggression can be impulsive, elicited by anger in response to provocation known as reactive or hostile aggression, or it can be premeditated, less emotional, and used to obtain some other end (known as proactive or instrumental aggression). Despite their different surface characteristics, these aggression instantiations all conform to the scholarly definition of aggression as behavior intended to cause harm to someone who is motivated to avoid that harm. Men can misinterpret aggressive women as too much of a challenge to handle, but in many cases, if they are in a loving relationship, a man can respond very well to aggressive women. In spanking, though, the woman is doing the spanking—an activity showing aggression—if there is consent and the man wants it, the aggressive woman can be a major turn on, which can be very attractive to men.

Males generally have higher testosterone levels and are more aggressive than females. Similarly, because men are more violent than women globally and possess much higher testosterone concentrations than women, researchers suspected that testosterone is a strong cause of aggression in men. However, much less research has investigated this possibility in women. One study of 87 women inmates in a maximum-security prison found that testosterone levels correlated with aggressive dominance. This relationship was reduced among older women, presumably due to lower levels of testosterone.

Similarly, a study of a women's rugby team found that the pre-game rise in testosterone was positively correlated with aggressiveness during the game. Another correlational study measured testosterone in 155 men and 151 undergraduate women. Men reported greater aggression and had five times more testosterone than the women. Despite these mean differences, the authors found positive correlations between testosterone and self-reported aggression in both women and men. Although aggression and testosterone may be lower in women than men, many studies observed the same positive relationships between testosterone and aggression in women as they do in men. This means that strong, confident and aggressive women are interesting to men because they can relate to these women who take charge readily and show very similar traits as strong confident men. So, men can relate to the power of a confident, strong woman and respect her as his Queen because she is his woman.

Marisa Rudder

CHAPTER 7

Tools for Spanking

There are a variety of tools available that are considered the best for fun spanking sessions, including the hand, paddle, tawse, strap, hairbrush, feather duster or belt. Other popular ones are canes, riding crops, whips, switches, birches sneakers, phonebooks, rolled-up catalogs or newspapers, rulers or martinets.

The Paddle

A spanking paddle is one of the most popular tools for spanking. It is mostly used to strike a person on the buttocks as this has been found to be an erotic zone. The act of spanking a person with a paddle is known as "paddling." Paddles are made of wood or plastic. Paddles were used in schools for punishment so people who like spanking may want that feeling of being disciplined. It is believed that the paddle may have originally been used for the punishment of slaves to cause intense pain without doing any permanent damage.

So, it makes its way into the sexual experience when the master uses the paddle to spank the sex slave. This can be a man or a woman, but in the Female Led Relationship, the woman will often do the spanking and the man is the submissive. Different types of paddles will have different sensations. Rigid paddles will likely hurt less than many flexible paddles. Paddles made from faux fur are going to feel almost like a massage, while a paddle made from silicone, wood, or hard leather will provide an intense feeling. It's probably best to start with light and progress to intense. A large paddle will likely feel like it hurts less than a paddle that only strikes a concentrated area.

The Flogger

Floggers are great to use once you start with the paddle and you want to progress. One step past the paddles, you'll find the floggers. Once many beginners have tried out paddles, they're eager to try the flogger. Floggers consist of multiple strands of a long, string-like material attached to a handle. When swung, the tips of these strands should hit the designated target. Floggers can feel like a massage or it can inflict a great amount of pain. It all depends on the way the flogger is made and how it is used. Heavier floggers are likely to create a massaging sensation, while lighter ones are likely to be a bit more painful. Soft materials, such as suede or faux fur, will offer a gentler feeling, while harsher materials, like unsoftened leather or rubber, will deliver a sharper strike with a lot more bite.

How to Use It

The flogger requires a coordinated motion of the wrist to allow the tips of the flogger's tails to touch an intended point on the receiver's body. This can include rolling the wrist, a gentle back and forth motion, and many other gestures. It's imperative you practice these movements on inanimate objects before you move onto using them on a partner. While it may look easy at first, aiming a flogger can be difficult, and you don't want to accidentally hit a part of the body that is bony. Start with a gentle flogger, such as one made from faux fur until you perfect your technique.

The Tickler

Ticklers are sensation-inducing items and are usually attached to the top of long rods so they can be used from a distance. Sensation-inducing items include soft suede strands, feathers, metal beads, rubber strands, and more. Ticklers can feel soft and gentle on the skin—and usually leads to tickling and laughing. When used a bit more roughly, ticklers can leave a stinging sensation and leave marks on the skin.

How to Use It

To use a tickler for tickling, use a light hand and run the tickler softly across your partner's skin. Try to choose areas that are more sensitive for better results. While ticklers are primarily used for tickling, these small, portable items can be used for impact play as well. Instead of using the tickler in a dragging motion, use it in more of a spanking fashion. Be careful not to touch sensitive areas like eyes or ears. You don't want the fibers to end up irritating the body. Stick to large, fleshy areas. Start with soft gentle tickles with your tickler and then mix in a light tap with the plastic of the tickler rod. Get several types and get your partner to choose which one he wants, then touch his skin with the different ones.

The Riding Crop

The riding crop is mostly used in equestrian sports as an encouragement tool and are long, flexible rods with a unique tip at the end. It's a mixture of a cane and a paddle. The tip of a riding crop produces the most sensation. Depending on how much force is put behind the strike, it can feel particularly painful—or it can feel like a gentle tap. The amount of force behind the strike makes a huge difference. Light taps and lightly touching the skin can be teasing, while direct taps can produce more pain.

How to Use It

To produce the two different sensations, you'll need to strike the skin with different forces. To be softer, just use the tip gently, but to produce more pain, then a more forceful strike will create a very painful sensation. Alternatively, you can use the flexible rod of the riding crop much like you'd use a cane. Be aware that many riding crops can feel as intense as a cane when used in this manner.

CHAPTER 8

Basics of Spanking

T he basics of spanking involve establishing consent, creating an agreement, planning the event, preparing costumes, tools and the scene, then allowing it to unfold in a safe, sexy, and fun intimate way. The actual act of spanking is striking your man for the sexual arousal or gratification for both of you. It may involve very light and brief spanking or a much more extensive session, including the use of implements, such as whips or paddles.

Activities range from a spontaneous smack on bare buttocks during sexual activity to occasional sexual role-play, such as age-play, or domestic discipline and may involve the use of a hand or a variety of spanking implements, such as a spanking paddle or cane. The paddle is the tool used to strike your partner on the buttocks. The act of spanking a person with a paddle is known as "paddling."

When we refer to dominance and submission in BDSM, we're talking about consensual power exchange. Meaning that even if your man, a submissive partner, is tied up and allows the dominant partner, the Queen, to dictate what happens, the terms have been discussed and agreed upon by both beforehand. Respect your man's limits. Before trying anything new, talk it over with him to make sure you're both into whatever is about to happen. Communication is part of having good sex. The willingness to talk about the kind of sex we have or want to have is a key skill.

Kate McCombs, a sex and relationships educator, states, "When you avoid those vital conversations, you might avoid some awkwardness, but you're also settling for suboptimal sex." By having these conversations, you and your partner's relationship can have emotional, psychological, and mental benefits. Sexual likes and dislikes can run on a spectrum. There are activities you love, ones you can't even think about, and all the stuff in between. And what happens to things that you haven't even heard of yet? Or when your desires change? Communicating such intimate needs requires a high-level of confidence and trust. At the same time, communication builds confidence and trust. Think about what you would be comfortable with and what makes you uncomfortable. Communicating these needs with your partner helps keep things open. Spanking can be virtually new and unfamiliar territory. Buried emotions can emerge, so discussing how you and your man feel about adding spanking to your sex lives— as well as brainstorming any unforeseen consequences and how you will deal with them—is important.

Erotic spankings are commonly combined with other forms of sexual foreplay. All acts must be consensual, and the scene should be pre-negotiated. It's very important to establish a safe word. For instance, "yellow" is often used to mean "slow down" and "red" to mean "stop." You may be interested in choosing a safe word that stops play if needed. Adhering to the safe word and respecting it is crucial. Learning each other's turn-ons and boundaries are all part of the fun of BDSM.

During spanking, it's also important to only hit fleshy areas with a good amount of fat and muscle. So, when spanking, you should focus on the meatiest part of your partner's behind. Try to go as low as you can without actually hitting the leg. It is important to go low in order to be able to stimulate the genital region successfully with every hit. Use your partner's reactions to find out if it's actually working and to what extent. You will have to use the same principle to find the perfect amount of force used. Unless he directly demands it, don't ever spank so hard that you leave a trace. Another important thing to remember is to take off any jewelry you might have as it can cause unwanted injuries.

It is best to try to increase blood flow to an area to make it really sensitive and as pleasurable as possible, so a feather tickler is a great way to create that pins-and-needles type feeling across someone's skin. They'll then be really sensitive to kisses and licks and tickles, and all the things that follow.

Begin very slow getting feedback all along. How is he doing? Is he enjoying it? Is it too much? The Queen should start with the hand, then move to other tools, like the paddle or flogger. It is important to keep a watch on how your partner is enjoying it. If you're in a relationship, you can initiate discussions early on about spanking and raise the idea of trying it before actually doing it. If you're dating someone casually, it is important to figure out if it's something you want to engage in early on. Ensure you have consent—even if you have been married for a long time. Consent means the ability to stop a sexual encounter at any moment, including changing their mind.

Dr. Dulcinea Pitagora, also known as the "King Doctor," is a licensed psychotherapist and sex therapist who focuses on providing affirmative, sex-positive therapy to those with atypical sexual and gender expressions. Dr. Pitagora has also been a member of the NYC kink scene for more than a decade and formerly worked as a professional dominatrix.

She defines sexual spanking as performed in the context of a role-play. The reality is that no one is actually getting punished for anything. It's part of a scene that you've already negotiated. The goal is mutual pleasure. You're experiencing it because the person doing the spanking enjoys spanking, and the person being spanked likes to be spanked.

In Female Led Relationships, couples will take it a little further. The importance of male obedience in this relationship cannot be overstated, so many couples enjoy using spanking as punishment, and some Queens will spank a man to tears. Men admit to being turned on when he submits completely to this degree of spanking. When a man submits, he is also admitting that he respects his woman and her decisions. He knows that when he is punished, it is never out of anger but out of love from the Queen. All men are not the same, and some men can take a lot while others will cry with hardly any swats administered. In the Female Led Relationship, the Queen rules and administers the spanking. Once there is consent, she decides how much and when to stop—unless the man uses his safe word.

Spanking can bring out a man's submissive side and breaks down his resistance and shame from being in a vulnerable position, naked over his Queen's lap, being spanked. Spanking is part of a man's submission, and when he submits to such an obviously painful and humbling experience, he will behave better and his attitude toward the Queen is greatly improved— not because he is fearful of the spanking—but out of respect and the knowledge that you are now more powerful than he is, and you will protect him from himself and his bad actions.

Giving discipline to a misbehaving man is not cruelty, it is love. And in a Female Led Relationship, the more you teach a man to behave properly, the more loving ensues. The Queen must take the lead in discussions and in administering the act.

It is essential that the Queen respects how much her man is willing to take and how long it takes him to fully commit. Both partners should take time to warm up. So, add in spanking gradually. Spanking should be an appetizer, not the main course.

In a Female Led Relationship, the Queen may decide to spank first where she is in control, followed by oral sex where her man takes over and finally intercourse. As the submissive, and loyal servant knight of the Queen, her man is expected to follow her lead. If she wants to use the tickler before the cane, then this is her decision, and within the limits of how much her man can take. As the leader of the Love & Obey movement, I have seen how spanking and discipline can transform couples and their sex lives. I know women are superior and must have complete and absolute obedience from men. I believe discipline helps men recognize female authority over them and creates submission. Men must be taught to be obedient and submissive to women.

Marisa Rudder

CHAPTER 9

How to Use Spanking as Part of a FLR

S panking is growing in popularity, but it becomes an extremely powerful act in a Female Led Relationship. Here, the Queen is the ruler and the man follows. Does this mean that spanking becomes punishment? No, spanking represents a new opportunity for both men and women to explore their needs. Men in Female Led Relationships want to submit. Since spanking is only done with consent, it means that only if the man is willing should the couple explore it. So, it gives men the opportunity to learn to submit and empowers the Queen to have the control.

Two transformative things can happen. Men, who are so accustomed to having all the power, are free to explore being led and serving a Queen. I saw this in the popular series *Game of Thrones*. Many of the male characters eventually learn the joy of serving the Queen after spending years chasing power. The character of Theon Greyjoy tried to take Winterfeld only to submit to his sister as Queen and later serve Lady Sansa, Lady of Winterfell once she takes back the throne. John Snow, happily head of the Knights Watch, falls for the Queen

Daenerys Targaryen and pledges his life to serving her even over love and becoming King on the Iron Throne.

FLR couples will use the idea of discipline as the way in which the Queen disciplines the man for his transgressions or disobedience. If the Queen feels disrespected, she can suggest ten lashes during the spanking session in bed. Or she can just decide that a stand-alone spanking session is necessary. Another approach is to spank the man for a set period of time for a specific offense. So, for example, a man might be spanked for five minutes for a simple case of male bad behavior, such as being disrespectful to his Queen by swearing at her or verbally raising his voice or talking back to her. For a more serious offense, such as getting drunk and not fulfilling his basic responsibility to maintain the home in a reasonable state of cleanliness, he might be spanked for a good half hour. Since the man receives a set punishment for a set offense, these approaches are quite simple and straightforward.

Both the Queen and her man must agree on the spanking because even in a Female Led Relationship, consent is still needed. It is also important to have consistency. Since FLR helps to train a man to be submissive to his Queen, like all other training, it is crucial to be consistent. If the Queen decides that spanking is the punishment, then later at night when both of you are tired, you cannot opt out or omit the act. It must be carried out so that the Queen is taking consistent control and her man is learning to submit.

In FLR, once you start adding spanking to your lifestyle, spanking is an exhilarating sexual fantasy, and it will boost your lovemaking. Most couples agree that the female led lifestyle is much more sexual than a patriarchal lifestyle and much more congruent for spanking your man. It is very difficult to allow your man to be in charge daily, then want him to be submissive while you spank him. Most patriarchal relationships will generally not be able to handle a woman spanking her man, and as a result, will not be truly submissive to her.

In a Female Led Relationship, the focus is on female pleasure. The sex is for the female first, and this makes the process of discipline and spanking so much more powerful. Women are as sexual as men, and men should provide them with erotic pleasure and orgasms. We strongly encourage all men to become experts at performing oral sex for women and support women as they explore their sexual desires without guilt, blame or judgment. We also know that our female desire to engage in spanking comes out of our need for attention. Love & Obey recognizes women as lusty and urges men to value the Queen's erotic pleasure above their own. We also advise men to make love so that the woman enjoys her climaxes first, and that men are only allowed to climax with his woman's permission. We encourage cuddling, kissing, and playful sensual touch to heighten a woman's arousal, alongside the discipline and spanking.

In FLR, both the Queen and her man agree that spanking is punishment for disobedience, dishonesty and disrespect, but the Queen then has the responsibility of deciding whether a man's bad behavior constitutes disobedience, dishonesty or disrespect. If the Queen decides that the man's bad behavior constitutes one of those three, and is therefore punishable, the Queen will then decide how severely he needs to be punished. If the Queen makes the decision, then it is final. There are less arguments, which makes for a smoother and more loving disciplinary process. It increases the man's opportunities to submit to his Queen, rather than to debate with her. It increases his chances of receiving the discipline he deserves and needs. It increases his chances of learning his lesson about his unruly behavior. It reduces the emotional stress that the Queen experiences as a result of not only having to spank him for bad behavior, but also for having to debate about whether he actually deserves to be punished or not.

CHAPTER **10**

The Best Positions for Spanking

S panking positions will vary according to the physical attributes of both the Queen and her man. If she is tall and strong, she may prefer different positions, and may use various tactics than a woman who is smaller and weaker. Physicality on its own will not determine the Queen's desire to try all positions, just some may be more comfortable. I encourage you both to try all and see what works. Variety is the spice of life, so don't be afraid to add your own modifications.

Here is a list of the best spanking positions:

1. Standing

There is no positioning involved. The Queen who is doing the spanking simply approaches her man from behind and hits his bottom. This is used mostly for impromptu, short spankings to deliver a quick warning to him, which works well for punishment or discipline in an ongoing dominant/submissive relationship. However, most people do not like to be surprised with a spanking, so doing this needs to be negotiated beforehand. If consensual, the surprise factor creates vulnerability and embarrassment. Pain is also higher when you are unprepared for it. Sometimes the Queen can spank her man in passing as a fun little surprise tap. I always suggest that if your man disrespects you or misbehaves, a little spanking on his butt **while** around the house does wonders. First, it reminds him of who is in charge, and second, it helps to address the issue without getting too serious.

This is an interesting position for role-playing, which sets the mood. You are the headmistress, and he has been a bad schoolboy. Or he is the criminal and you are the naughty police officer. Maybe he needs to be up against a wall and spread 'em. Don't underestimate the power of teasing.

2. Bound and Blindfolded

If your man is bound and blindfolded, everything is a surprise, and he has no idea what's coming next. I always suggest lying face up, sitting up or standing. Never place a man face down as it could affect his breathing. The blindfold is the element of surprise whether you're going to go hard or soft, fast or slow. He also can't see what instrument you're going to use, so really feel free to play. It's also fun to watch them tense when they feel nothing but the breeze coming from a paddle you might be waving near the target area, or they hear the swoosh of a cane as you flick it through the air. Adding sensory deprivation to your sex life is an easy and tantalizing way to build tension. When you temporarily subtract stimuli from one sense, you can heighten others. For instance, when you can't see because you're wearing a blindfold, a whisper in your ear or the taste of your partner's mouth may seem all the more intense—and exciting.

If you want to buy a blindfold, start with a comfy silk scarf. You can also use a sleeping mask or the silk tie of a bathrobe. Depending on what role you want to play, ask your partner to blindfold you or ask if you can blindfold them. Once the blindfold is on, the partner not wearing it can tease and tantalize the wearer, leaving them guessing what's coming next by kissing all over their body, whispering dirty talk into their ear, or tickling erogenous zones with a feather.

3. Bent Over Furniture

The Queen can stand in this act, but the man is bent over a desk, a table, or the back of an armchair. Alternatively, he is made to kneel over the edge of the bed, over a chair, or to kneel on a chair. In public play spaces, there are spanking benches specially created for this position. With most furniture, the Queen can press her left (non-dominant) hand over the lower back of her man to add a bit of restraint. Being bent over a piece of furniture is mildly embarrassing. In this position, there is lots of room to swing the arm and the Queen can really put her weight into it to gain more force. This position is very comfortable for your man. The main drawback is that there is no physical contact with the Queen's body, creating an emotional distance.

4. Over the Lap

This is the classical spanking position. The Queen sits on a chair or on the edge of the bed, and the man is face down over her lap. He is over the thighs of the Queen and in contact with her lower belly. The great attributes about this position are the psychological effect of the mental image it creates, the contact with the Queen's body, and the fact that the butt is lifted and exposed in all its beautiful roundness. The main drawback of this position is that it is not a comfortable position for the man if he is large and heavy since he will tend to roll off the lap. Also, the Queen finds it easier to hit the buttock that is farthest from his belly, creating an uneven spanking. He can mimic a similar position lying face down on a sofa while the Queen is on a chair.

5. Over the Knee

The 'over the knee' position is where the man lies on the Queen's leg with his hands and feet on the floor. This position can also be done if the Queen sits on a bed, preferably with her back supported by the head of the bed. This way, the man can rest his full body on the bed, which is more relaxing and stable. On a bed, the man can be moved away from the lap and onto the knees proper; this way, his bottom is farther from the Queen's body, who can now hit both buttocks more evenly. This is a great position for long spankings because it is comfortable and effortless for both the Queen and her man and has more body contact than bending over furniture.

However, the man has to turn his head sideways to breathe. It is less embarrassing than other positions and only moderately vulnerable. Another drawback is that there is no restraint, and a feisty man can struggle and move around with ease. Restraint can be increased by holding a hand of the man over his lower back, or by using bondage. This is a very sexy position as he is automatically in a position of weakness. As a woman, you can now go to town with your flogger or paddle, and he must lie there and take it. This can be very arousing for men. For added intensity, bound his hands together, then get him over your legs.

A variation of this that I personally love is lying on a coffee table. Feel free to tie his hands to the table on a cushion to support his penis. Now you have ample ability to use any tool. Sometimes I like to tie up my partner and leave him there to contemplate his bad behavior, then I return to administer punishment.

6. Straddling the Leg

This is a variant of the 'over the lap' position that is very popular with the domestic discipline crowd. The man is made to straddle the thigh of his Queen who is sitting on a chair or on the edge of the bed. Then the man leans forward and is held in position with the left arm of the Queen. Holding one hand of the man on his lower back and wrapping the right leg of the Queen over the man's left calf can restrain her almost completely. This is quite an embarrassing and vulnerable position because it spreads the legs, exposing the anus. If it's a woman experiencing this, her clit will be stimulated during the spanking, creating a deeply sexual experience. This is a great position to spank a woman to orgasm. Cumming while being spanked is quite a mental trip. If it's the man, the effects on his cock and balls can vary from pleasurable to painful. In any case, the body contact is great, the restraint is nice, and the Queen can hit both buttocks forcefully and evenly. Lack of back support for the Queen may be a main problem, but this can be solved by sitting in an armchair.

7. Man Table

This position can be easily created with the man kneeling on all fours like a table. The Queen sits on the sofa and can be bent over. This position is great because the Queen is free to move around as she pleases. She can place her feet up on his back for added fun.

The drawback for "man table" is that if your man has a back problem, then it could be uncomfortable.

8. Sitting on or Straddling the Man

The wrestling spanking is a fun game in which the man does not submit to the spanking but has to be wrestled and immobilized by the Queen. This may also require that the man is immobilized throughout the spanking so that he cannot escape. One way to achieve this is to sit straddling his lower back. To get away, the man would need to pull up his weight and that of the Queen, which for most people is impossible. It is also difficult for him to turn over or to protect his bottom with his hands, because the Queen's body blocks the way. Hence, the man has to endure his punishment until the Queen decides to stop, which makes for high vulnerability and embarrassment. The main problem is that a heavy Queen may injure the man's back, therefore, this needs to be given careful consideration. Otherwise, it is a very domineering position for a spanking.

9. Wheelbarrow Position

This is the most exposed and humiliating position for a spanking. The Queen sits on a sofa or an armchair and the man places his legs up around her hips. His hands are on the floor and he is balanced with his hips up. The buttocks can now be spanked like playing a drum. If the Queen desires, then she can have her man hold this position for quite a while. This can be great for a very athletic man but much harder for one who is not as strong. The turn on is that this is a very vulnerable position so the man with his butt in the air can be stimulated. This position would be great for shorter positions.

CHAPTER **11**

What Does It Mean to Be Submissive?

There is a beautiful surrender that comes when a man allows himself to be vulnerable and submissive. When negative life experiences harden a man, a strong Female Led Relationship can help men to relax their rigid boundaries. Hundreds of thousands of men are embracing a female led lifestyle. Why? Because they find joy in being a submissive man to a strong woman. The assumption is that submissive men give up all responsibility for themselves, are doormats that cannot stand up for themselves, and so are taken advantage of by predatory dominant Queens, but this couldn't be further from the truth. Submissives are stereotypically extremely strong, capable men. Many of them crave submission as a way to temporarily escape the huge responsibilities they take on in their normal lives.

The subspace is important for submissives. In BDSM, subspace refers to a specific kind of space with its own rules, texture, and properties—a kind of altered reality. In BDSM, this altered reality usually takes place in the mind, although changes in the surrounding physical space can make a difference as well. This is why, for instance, people go out of their way to set up private playrooms. These intentionally designed settings make it easier to get into the mood of an interaction—to enter a psychological state where all the worries, cares, underlying thoughts, and emotions are stripped away, and your deepest, darkest fantasies can become reality.

The "subspace" we're talking about is the specific psychological state of mind that the submissive partner enters into during a scene with a dominant partner. To enter this subspace, the sub must be completely comfortable with the dominant, as they completely give up control to the Queen. In many ways, getting into a subspace follows many of the same steps of practicing basic mindfulness; you must be 100 percent present with your partner and in the moment.

Subspace is that feeling of utter presence when all of your senses are heightened, and your mind and emotions are totally wrapped up in the suspense of the moment. For the submissive man, entering subspace is an experience that melts away all their worries and fears. They don't have to think about anything or make any tough decisions. All they need to do is obey and go with the flow. On a psychological level, the point of this kind of exchange is to make the sub feel that the scene is real, thereby triggering their sympathetic nervous system into the "fight or flight" response. Most submissive men agree that when a session is over, they feel a sense of euphoria, a warm, ecstatic glow. It can be such an intense, natural high that subs can feel as though they are walking two feet off the ground.

The afterglow, for the submissive man can last for hours, even weeks. It creates feelings of love, attachment, belonging, and well-being, and the man and the dominant Queen also share a special connection, in that they know a side of each other that others are completely unaware of. This makes them intimate in a way that others cannot know or understand. Psychologically, this sort of play is very healing too. Submissive men usually can carry with them sexual desires that they feel they must hide away. But this allows them a free space to explore those fantasies without fear of judgment. A loving female authority who is in charge works for submissive men, and they find them tremendously sexy and attractive.

There is so much to the psychology of spanking when it comes to surrender. Much of the pleasure and arousal is generated in our erotic desires, fantasies, and memories in the G-spots of our minds. When spanking involves role-play, it entails dominance and submission. The dynamics of power and surrender. Dominance and submission fantasies are pervasive in society and nature. They can be crude or romantic, marvelous, or dangerous. They may involve sadomasochism, bondage and discipline, spanking as playful punishment, an imagined abduction or a "maintenance" spanking, over-the-knee paddling, whipping, flogging or caning. The setting for a spanking fantasy could be a childhood home, boarding school, boudoir, church or temple, office, party, military barracks, POW camp, the great outdoors, heaven, hell, or another planet.

The trust between the man and his Queen is so incredible that when he gives himself up to her entirely, it is almost like an out of body experience. He is in "subspace." Reality melts away and nothing matters but her next move, her next command. He focuses on the Queen's voice, her touch, and he yearns to serve her. A lot of submission comes from psychological dominance. The role of dominant, or master, or daddy, is ultimately to care for their sub, to nurture and to guide them, and to help them reach their full potential for both his pleasure and for hers.

Marisa Rudder

CHAPTER **12**

Effects of Spanking on the Body

S panking is very exciting, and one of the effects on the body is a release of endorphins, which are responsible for happy feelings. The sensation of a hand hitting your skin can cause an adrenaline surge as additional blood flows to the surface of the skin, making all of the nerve receptors in the skin more sensitive, enhancing the sensation of a caress. The BDSM community refers to this as being a sensual experience, which shuts down the activity in your frontal cortex. It can be immensely helpful for overactive thinkers, which is why aggressive type A male personalities enjoy this. It almost calms them down.

On a physiological level, the fear element gets the adrenal glands going, flooding the system with epinephrine, followed by endorphins. Epinephrine, also known as adrenaline, energizes us when we are in the thick of "danger." Once we know the danger is over, the endorphins kick in. These are the body's natural painkillers, and they model opioids in how they make us feel by relaxing us and giving us a sense of calm and well-being.

A study from 2009 found that couples who engaged in positive, consensual sadomasochistic activity had lower levels of the harmful stress hormone cortisol, and also reported greater feelings of relationship closeness and intimacy after their sexual play. And a preliminary study of a handful of "switches," like people who take on the opposite role they're used to, such as a Dom who becomes a sub, found that consensual BDSM can reduce anxiety by bringing the mind to an altered "flow" state of consciousness. This is similar to the feeling some get when they experience a "runner's high," engage in creating art, or practice yoga.

From attraction to action, sexual behavior takes many forms. At least for humans, this most basic of activities is anything but basic. As the pioneering sex researcher Alfred Kinsey put it, the only universal in human sexuality is variability itself. People normally engage in sexual activity for any number of reasons—to feel alive, to maintain a vital aspect of human functioning, to feel desirable and attractive, to achieve closeness, or to please a partner they love. Spanking adds an element of adventure and excitement to a routine sex life. The pleasure of sex arises from many factors including the release of neurochemicals, such as oxytocin and dopamine, which flood the system during orgasm, as well as the sense of connection communicated by touching.

According to Dr. Becky Spelman, a psychologist and clinical director of the Private Therapy Clinic, the reason for our appreciation of spanking is both physical and emotional. Classical conditioning is the automatic response to prior learning. For example, spanking can be linked to something you've experienced in the past. Dr Spellman says, "It usually occurs around a particular traumatic episode, which is then stamped into the child's psyche." Spanking can cause a lot of shame in childhood, and rather than holding on to the shame, it's common for people to later in life turn the traumatic experience into a sexual one to help cope with what they have experienced, leading to a strong emotional connection between spanking and sex, which now manifests as a fetish.

When we're stressed or in pain, our brains release numerous chemicals: endorphin, serotonin, melatonin, epinephrine, norepinephrine, and dopamine. And not just physical pain but emotional and social discomfort as well—all for the purpose of rebalancing our bodies and trying to make us feel good again. One of the key players is dopamine, which is present in the body during pain and pleasure. Many agree this might be one of the reasons we can combine pain and pleasure in a single situation. Spanking causes all of this to go on in our bodies at the same time. For your man, as a submissive after the initial opiate-like euphoria wears off, many subs feel what's often called a "drop" or a "subdrop." This is when the biochemicals begin to taper off, leaving a sleepy, relaxed feeling in their place. At this point, what's known as "aftercare," in which the sub's physical and emotional needs are seen to, is very important. After the exertion of play, for instance, a blanket or robe may be needed since the body temperature often drops from the sudden stoppage of energy.

The reason for the spanking is because when it is done on the butt, its proximity to the sex organs makes it part of the overall sexual feeling. During spanking, the gluteal muscles are often squeezed together, which researchers have found is similar to what happens during orgasm. Sexual peaks are achieved when blood flow increases and collects in key hot spots or erogenous zones.

In the case of the male, the proximity of the buttocks to the scrotum and the penis is an important factor and seems to contribute to the erection. Blood rushing to the spanked bottom causes the male sexual organs to swell, much as they do in preparation for the orgasm. An additional anatomical element in sexual response to spanking is the fact that the anal opening shares some muscles with the perineum—a very erogenous area between the anus and the genitalia. During the course of most spankings, this area comes into contact with either the hand or the tool used to strike the buttocks.

Occasionally, depending on the size of the paddle or spanking implemented, the sexual organs will be accidentally struck—this can happen with either gender as the recipient. While no damage is sustained, an immediate sexual response is often the result. One phenomenon is the apparent fact that the sexual feelings induced by a spanking are either stronger than or blot out the presence of pain. While there may be some physical discomfort, it adds to the eroticism of this activity, rather than detracting.

The Thrill of the Spank

The emotional and psychological aspects of pain and pleasure involve submission, which is the giving up control to another person; humiliation, a form of psychological pain; sexual objectification, the sexual value of the body as an object; and role-playing, which involves participating in sexual fantasies.

Whether it's good for the man or not, psychologically speaking, some people just like to give a good spanking. Power is a rush, in fantasy and reality, and spanking, even at a birthday party, gives you a certain power—the power to hurt, humiliate, heal, or stimulate. Of course, power corrupts, especially in real life, where many people pursue physical power over others, often entering politics, police, or military careers, "spanking" the populace with punitive laws and sadistic punishments, not to mention "spanking" smaller, relatively defenseless countries with bombs.

Others prefer to keep their power trips in their erotic imaginations or perhaps act them out through real life role-play. Some cultivate spanking as an art, deriving as much creative pleasure from giving a good spanking as a musician might from playing an instrument. And yes, there's a fine line between making music and making love—and no, it's not just because one of my favorite forms of spanking is Butt Bongo.

Dominance is traditionally considered a male prerogative, so it is most popular among young men who are relatively powerless in real-life society—perhaps by choice, though usually they may not even have any testosterone-pumping energy to spare. But more and more women are saying that they enjoy being dominant, "on top," and wielding a whip or even sprouting a penis (okay, Freud was right about some women having "penis envy"). This "penis" could be the obvious strap-on dildo, which many dominant women enjoy sporting, but the penis substitute could also be a phallic foot (as in the Bible, where the foot, leg or thigh is often used as a euphemism for the forbidden-to-pronounce male sex organ), or a hand, paddle, whip or flogger.

Often as subtle as it is predictable, desire is part biology, part psychology, and takes shape differently in men and women. For men, arousal typically precedes desire. But for women, desire precedes arousal, in response to physical intimacy, emotional connection, and an atmosphere free of distractions and everyday concerns. Scientists are continuously exploring the interplay of biological influences, such as neurohormones that suppress or enhance desire, and psychological influences, such as emotions and relationships. Spanking affects a man's arousal, which leads to more desire of his Queen to control him, which eventually also leads to both being more turned on.

Indeed, besides so-called disciplinary, erotic, and sensual spanking, there is also therapeutic spanking, or "spanking therapy," which is employed for its curative effects. The therapeutic power of a spanking or flogging may be primarily physical, like a good massage or brisk rubdown, but spanking therapy can also be deeply psychological, releasing the man being spanked from all kinds of stress, guilt, shame, and tension, with much of it stemming from childhood. The best spanking therapy breaks through destructive, debilitating mental and sexual blocks, improving the mental well-being of both the man getting spanked and his Queen.

In 2005, a team of Russian scientists led by Sergei Speransky found "whipping therapy" to be an effective prophylaxis against alcohol and drug abuse, depression, suicidal thoughts, and psychosomatic diseases, due to the release of endorphins during and after spanking. Dr. Speransky recommends 30 sessions of 60 whip lashes on the buttocks in every session for maximum therapeutic effect. Today, the Queen spanking her man even during sex can serve as therapy.

CHAPTER **13**

Why Couples Love Role-Playing

Role-play during sex involves acting out a sexual fantasy. It may be done during foreplay or it can be the main event. According to the 2015 Sexual Exploration in America Study, more than 22 percent of sexually active adults engage in role-playing. Couples love role-play as a chance to spice things up and try new things or be someone else. This tends to be sexually arousing because suddenly you and your partner can perform acts out of the norm. Spanking presents a perfect time to use role-play because the Queen becomes a character who is spanking her man as the submissive character. Some couples become so involved in role-play they insist on elaborate costumes and scripts. Many fetish parties will act out role-playing fantasies, but they can just as easily be done at home.

Nearly any role could become the base material for an erotic experience, and there is no limit to what objects an individual could consider sexual. It may, for example, involve wearing a costume that is regarded as erotic, such as a miniskirt and stockings, or one or both partners being nude, say for an evening. It may involve elements of dominance and submission, passivity, or obedience. It may involve sexual bondage, with either partner being restrained. Bondage plus spanking go together perfectly.

Another element that makes sexual role-play appealing is that the concept of it not just about the physical act of getting off. It's actually just as stimulating for the mind as it is for the body.

When the Queen and her man are able to truly let go in order to fulfill their deepest fantasies in the form of role-playing, it taps right into the imagination, which, in turn, creates an even sexier physical experience.

Some of the exciting role-playing games include:

1. Doctor or nurse and patient

2. Teacher and student

3. Escort and Client

4. Boss and Employee

5. Housewife and handyman (plumber or carpenter)

6. Master and slave

7. Photographer and Model: this allows one partner to photograph the other as a precursor to sexual interaction.

8. Female villain and James Bond

9. CIA agent and criminal

10. Strangers in a bar

Here are some tips on how to make your role-playing spectacular.

The best way to start something new is to discuss it with your partner, so you are both excited about it and can come up with fantasies that will stimulate both of you. You want to ensure you are both comfortable and willing to add it to your sex life. Not everyone likes to add new things to sex. There are many people who are quite happy with normal, so it is important to ensure both of you are eager. As the Queen in a Female Led Relationship, this may be something you wish to add to your sex sessions and your man is obligated to follow your lead. But it is important to respect his ideas as well. If it is the man who must convince the Queen, be respectful and make your suggestions but allow her to make the final decision. This is why communication becomes extremely important.

Role-playing doesn't need to be complicated. You can start out with doing some smaller and simpler things to get each other going. This could be wearing lingerie or trying out a sex toy. Heck, the two of you could even test out by speaking in some accents or using different props to begin with. Start simple and then move to complicated. Once you have done it a few times, then you can move to creating more complicated scenarios. This is the point when you can add spanking and combine the two. Remember, role-play should be fun. It may feel awkward and intimidating at first, but it's worth it to just try it out. The best way to figure out what works for you and your man is simply to try it out.

Marisa Rudder

CHAPTER **14**

How to Make the Perfect Torture Playroom

One of the greatest ways to make your spanking and sex sessions so much more exciting is to set up a playroom—*Fifty Shades of Grey* style. There is a reason we were so excited when Christian Grey led Ana into the most luxurious playroom. A sex playroom becomes a very special place for better sex, more relaxation, and a greater connection with your partner. A Queen can really feel like royalty in a playroom.

A playroom can enhance the sexiness of your sex and spanking sessions. In *Fifty Shades of Grey,* Christian has Ana sign contracts before entering the playroom, which had every type of equipment for play artistically laid out, resembling a kinky hotel room in Las Vegas. A bench with restraints, the cross, even a swing contraption has been used. The whips can range from a very sturdy paddle or leather flogger and whips. Some couples get into monogrammed restraints and very creative garb. One great example is the *Eyes Wide Shut* capes. The Goddess and her man wear these sumptuous capes until it's time to start spanking when then man drops his cape and bears his naked body.

Red and black are the most popular colors or something regal with rich purples, yellows, and blues. Lighting doesn't need to be dark, but it can be. Soft and romantic, harsh spotlights, or disco balls can all create a fun scene.

Here are some great sex dungeon toys, accessories, and furniture:

Sex Swing: A sex swing is such a great addition to a dungeon, and you don't have to fasten it to the ceiling with a large screw. There are some that are built to fit on a door jamb and are versatile enough to accommodate several different positions.

Blackout Mask: If you are not able to fully black out your windows, a blackout mask is a great way to create atmosphere and suspense. It's a great feature to keep hanging on your dungeon wall.

Cuffs: A dungeon just wouldn't be complete without having a set of handcuffs on hand to restrain your partner. If you have a bed, you can keep them near it. You can place your partner's wrists above their head. Better yet—if you are doing some bed play or even floor play, suction cuffs are an awesome option for restraint.

Collar and Leash: Your bottom/submissive might like to be led around by the collar in a session. In that case, you can install a hook on the wall and hang a collar and leash to use in your dungeon.

Spanking Paddle: Tools for pain play can be a big part of your dungeon play. There are so many to choose from, from whips to floggers to canes.

Storage: Choosing the right storage is important so you can have easy access to your tools and store them away carefully. One way to organize and store your tools when not using them is to install hooks on the walls of your dungeon. This not only helps keep you organized but having them out on display can set the psychological tone you may want for your submissive.

Here are some fun furniture you can add:

Spanking Bench

The spanking bench, or spanking horse, is a piece of furniture used to position your man on it, with or without restraints. Even celebrities like Cara Delevingne and Ashley Benson have reported buying and using a sex bench. Cara has previously hinted at an interest in BDSM during an interview on RuPaul's podcast *RuPaul: What's the Tee?* The spanking bench is similar to a sawhorse with a padded top and rings for restraints.

What's nice about it is that it allows the Queen to move around her subject easily, choosing to taunt and tease him from any angle. With restraints, it will ensure your man is held in place and he is comfortable. Some couples have these custom made with luxurious materials or just high-quality leather. It creates the ability to explore a multitude of sexual positions, and it can also be easily folded up and stored away since it is also designed to be discreet.

Sex Couch

A sex couch is the ultimate, classic sex lounge chair. It's designed so you can sit on it in a variety of ways so you can get that perfect position. Many come with straps and extra pillows to prop yourself up further or to have bondage furniture.

BDSM Bondage Board

Bondage frame boards and tables are adjustable so you can strap or rope a person to the board. This table has convenient holes with access points for the face, nipples, and genitals, and it is collapsible, so you can store it under the bed or in a closet. It makes for a great addition to any playroom.

Bondage Cross

A bondage cross is a standing fixture that allows you to strap someone in in a vertical position. It's a stark fixture for your burgeoning sex dungeon...or a very interesting, abstract sculpture in the living room that your Uncle Joe might ask about sometime. The cross above is designed with vinyl upholstery and hand-welded aluminum, so you're getting the top-of-the-line as far as bondage furniture is concerned.

Here are some added tips:

Choose furniture that is high-quality and well made, even if it's just one or two pieces. Make sure floors, walls, furniture, and other surfaces are easily cleaned and sanitized.

If you're going to use candles for wax play or just decoration, nearby fabrics should be flame retardant. Battery candles can be convincing enough if you want mood lighting without worrying about the fire department showing up. Carpeted floors might not be the best idea, especially if you're going to be dealing with sweat, drool, and other bodily functions. Area rugs are the go-to if you really want something soft under your feet. Wood items should be sanded to avoid splinters. It's important to keep your playroom safe, warm, comfortable, and clean.

Other Ways to Transform Your Bedroom

1. Make Your Bedroom Off Limits

Kids, in-laws, parents, friends and pets should not be allowed into your bedroom, and it should remain untouchable by the outside world. Here are some ways you can ensure this:

- Place a lock on your door.

- Put up blackout curtains.

- Keep your phones off and out of the room

- Make sure that there's no TV in the room

- Reserve your bedroom for sleep and for deeply connecting sexual intimacy.

2. Add Scents

Scented candles, flowers and scents are all great ways to enhance your bedroom and make it sexy. Try various scents on different nights to really spice things up. Whether you and your man wants to relax after a busy day at the office, or you both use them to wake up and energize your senses for sex and spanking, scents can make all the difference.

Essential oil diffuser, some lightly scented candles, scents and perfumes can all be great to enhance the mood. Make sure you choose them together.

3. Keep Your Bedroom at a Slightly Cooler Temperature

When it comes to the sexiness of your bedroom, the temperature definitely matters. If it's too cold, then it might limit the number of positions you can do, and the body does not warm up. If it's too hot, then it's uncomfortable for both of you. Sweating too much can kill the mood.

4. Massage Oils are Fun

Sensual massage is one of the most efficient ways to get out of your head and into your body while simultaneously connecting with your partner and engaging in some light foreplay. Massage oils can be used in between spanking as well as before and after. It's a luxurious way to add to the sensations of the sessions.

5. Get some sexy sheets

Nothing is a greater turn on than some really sexy sheets. Get a set of quality, high thread count sheets that you both will enjoy. Avoid buying white sheets because, believe it or not, white sheets show stains. Consider a sexy pattern or satin sheets so when you lie on it, they put you both in the mood.

6. Set Up a Great Music System

Music and sex both tap into very primal parts of our brain, which is why the two go so well together. It might sound like it has the potential to be cheesy...but don't knock it until you've tried it. The right music can add a whole new swagger to your mattress mambo. Choose whatever makes you feel the sexiest. Pick up a set of quality speakers and cue up your skillfully cultivated playlist, and let the sweet tunes carry you further into your body.

CHAPTER **15**

How to Begin Spanking

S everal factors contribute to a good spanking. Preparation is key. After consent is established, it is time to plan the act itself. The technique, positions, implements, costumes, role-play and setting the ambiance. The perfect spanking session consists of the following below.

Discussion and Communication

It's fun to be spontaneous, but it is best to discuss all aspects of this activity well in advance. It's respectful and gives both of you a chance to iron out details and be clear about likes and dislikes. Establish consent.

Discuss Role-Play

Spanking is made so much more interesting with role-play. What roles will you and your man like to play. Examples are:

- Police officer/Criminal

- Teacher/Student etc.

Roles make it much naughtier and adds an element of play.

Choose Your Safe Word

This can be anything but once your man shouts this word, all spanking must stop. It helps with safety and both of you can gauge how the spanking session is going.

Choose Your Position

Different positions offer opportunities for different sensations in spanking. Standing can be much more difficult than lying, but the sensation of a whip going up your leg is just so exciting, as it is going across your back while lying over your Queen's lap. Get creative, and choose a different position each day.

Focus on the Butt

First, the buttocks is the largest muscle in the body. Second, the butt is where many men can have more fat, so it can withstand impacts without any bones or protrusions getting banged up. Third, the butt has close proximity to the genitals. During sex and foreplay, a lot of blood courses through these areas; a sharp slap to the buttocks actually increases blood flow and, as a result, arousal. Light smacks on the butt during the day can be a sexy foreplay before the big event.

Warm Up

Begin with light taps and perfect technique. This helps to prepare your man and less likely to cause a shock, which could make him uncomfortable. The warm up is a great time to tease.

Build Anticipation and Make Him Beg for it

Start with light and intermittent lashes, then let him hear the whip and feel it moving along his body like a snake. Take a break between each swat or combination of swats. Graze your hand over your partner's genitals, rub your palm on their cheeks in a circular motion, or do nothing at all, leaving your sub to helplessly anticipate when and where the next impact will happen. The more you can tease him, the more he will beg for you to just do it.

Alternate Between Slaps and Squeeze

Slap, squeeze tease. A mixture of soft and stinging sensations will make for a more dynamic and memorable erotic spanking session. In between sets of spanks, change up patterns, alter your hand shape and power. Grab his butt and caress in between slaps.

Add Extras

Restrain him with furry handcuffs. Blow in his ears. Touch his neck. Make him give you oral sex in between spankings. Get him on all fours to be spanked on the butt, then run your whip along his tummy while he's blindfolded.

Aftercare

Allow him to cool down. Offer a drink of water, a soft warm blanket, and definitely some light caresses and hugs. Cuddle, lie together and have some intimate moments gazing at each other, basking in the wonderful endorphins.

People like different things, and the same is true for men and spanking. Some men do not tolerate much pain but enjoy the mild stinginess and warmth of light slaps. Others are in it for the pain, and can appreciate firmer spanks after a good warm up. This will need to be discussed and after practicing, you both can get into the swing of things. Some positions are better than others. It will be important to try them all, then choose what works for you and your partner. Some people cannot take being bent over a lap while blood rushes to their head or standing for very long periods of time. So, you and your man will discuss all of this to ensure you have done everything to prepare for a smooth fun session. Another important sensation is the physical contact between the bodies of the person getting spanked and the one who is spanking. Some positions have a lot of contact and even put pressure on the genitalia, leading to a deeply sexual spanking. However, some people may prefer a less intimate experience.

How to Warm Up Properly

It is important to warm up. The last thing you want to do is give your partner a shock by hitting too hard when he is not ready. Good foreplay will lead to hotter and more enjoyable sex for both of you, and the same is true for erotic spanking. You want to make sure that he's comfortable, relaxed and ready for the experience. Start off by just rubbing the butt either bare or clothed. This helps to get the circulation going. Rubbing, caressing, or massaging the butt gives your lover a feel-good sensation and leaves them wanting more. It's all about mixing pleasure with pain—pushing their limits and making them want more." While you're doing this, you can talk dirty, which will make him ease into the moment even deeper. The key here is to take your time and not to rush it.

Start by warming up the area by massaging and running your paddle or flogger gently up and down the body. Tap it lightly to get the blood going. This is also a great time to really observe if he is enjoying it. Plus, it can be very pleasing to watch a soft blush occur. Many men like to feel the woman's hand and even the sight of her nails can be a turn on. It's great for a few light taps, followed by a really hard one when they were least expecting it, then squeezing his butt and penis, running your nails up and down his body.

There are plenty of areas you can aim a good spanking to. Most popular is, of course, the bum. It's nice and soft, blushes quickly, and no one will see it if you're keen on getting spanked to a bruising point. Otherwise, people are keen on getting a swift caning to the tops of the back of the thigh. Other areas you can consider include the bottom of the feet, across the chest and on the hands if you're going for more of a corporal punishment feel. Floggers are great because they don't injure the skin and hurt too bad. For sound effects, the paddle is great.

Sex expert Sienna Sinclaire says, "Once you've massaged his bare-bottom, or clothed, it's time to add in some surprising smacks here-and-there to prep for the spanking session. Start off with light slaps, then work up to what they are comfortable with. Rotate between cheeks but always end with rubbing his bottom. Once they are more used to it, and can take a bit more pain, then rub and slap their bottom more than once but ending with a rub. This step is important because it makes this erotic experience more personal and intimate with your partner. Once you slap their butt after the rub, it immediately goes from pleasure to pleasurable pain with a slight good sting. Then going back to the rubbing after the slap, which helps to take the sting away, replacing it with pleasure again but leaving them wanting to feel that pleasurable sting again."

Try to finish every spank with a slow, sensual and thoughtful caress. Also, use the timing to your advantage. Do your best to be as irregular and spontaneous as possible. If you swing your hand when he's not expecting it, the sensation will be much more intense. Remember to combine spanking with other actions like kissing and caressing. Don't make him feel like he's actually being punished for something and keep reminding him that you're doing this for his pleasure.

Sinclaire also suggests to mixing sex with spanking. "If your lover wants you to spank them while they are fucking you missionary style, you can easily reach your hands around onto their butt and spank them with the same spank-and-rub pattern," Sinclaire says since. this is very erotic for both.

CHAPTER **16**

How to Begin Spanking

The first spanking session is always pivotal. It will determine if this is something you and your partner will enjoy, or it could be a disaster. So great care must be taken in consideration when attempting to add this act to your sex life. Once you have discussed it with your partner, set the boundaries and discussed how it will generally happen when you can go ahead and proceed. Don't forget the safe word.

Begin by telling your partner by confirming you want to do this and set the scene. Lay out your tools and make the scene sexy. Some couples like to start with a sexy sensual shower, then you can lead him to the bed and have him lay down. It is of great importance to make him feel comfortable. It is not advisable to eat a heavy meal before engaging in this practice. If your man is lying down on his stomach, which is the preferred beginner position—but be mindful of his breathing, then he could feel a lot of unwanted pressure.

Once he is comfortable, you can begin with a little caressing of his body, light stroking or some teasing. It is best to begin with your hand as you have the most control. Rubbing the area of his buttocks or legs before striking will help him to relax.

When you are starting out, focus only on fleshy areas like his butt. Once you have mastered the perfect striking, then you can switch it up. Start light. A few light taps followed by rubbing so he can gently get used to it. Allow him to make noises if it hurts so you can judge the level of pain.

Once you have established a good pattern, do it in numbers of four or five, then followed by rubbing and caressing. Do this until you feel you are both turned on and ready to do other things. The first spanking session should be followed by sex so that it becomes an enjoyable part of your overall experience. Keep it light and friendly.

Some things to remember is to discuss how he is feeling throughout. Is he having any emotional outbursts? Sometimes the first time spanking can cause strange emotions to arise. It is important to monitor how he feels.

Setting the Scene

Setting the scene for all types of sexual pleasure goes a long way to getting both of you in the mood, and it is equally important in spanking. The great thing about adding erotic spanking to you sex life is the fear and the thrill of the unknown. Most couples have never experienced it. So, seeing the paddle and whips laid out while you're looking seductive and sexy adds to the extreme excitement that the act can have. In *Fifty Shades of Grey,* the sight of the playroom was both scary and exciting, but it was the anticipation of what could happen, and these are the thoughts that will race through both of your minds.

After you set the scene, remove all distractions. There is nothing worse than being in mid strike when the phone will ring, kids or the dog runs in. These are unwanted distractions during sex, but during spanking, it becomes even more of a problem. Spanking requires concentration and a connection between you and your man. Distractions not only kill the mood, but they can cause you to lose concentration and injure your man unnecessarily. If you are using tools, you don't want it to accidentally go into his eye or hit him on his joints. Removal of distractions is crucial to a great spanking session.

Distractions include jewelry or anything that can get in the way. This includes rings, watches, bracelets, necklaces and headbands. The last thing you want is an unwanted injury. I can recall wearing very long earrings once and having it get caught on a pillow—almost ripping my ear off. Not fun.

Check your tools and make sure they are not falling apart. I can recall a friend telling me a story of fishing out her old riding crop that she used for riding to use on her man, only to have the whole thing unravel and break on the first lash and spraying fibers everywhere. Make sure the tools are handy. There is nothing worse than getting to the point of wanting to switch to a tool, and you have to rummage through your closet to find it. Yeah, he'll understand, but it's a mood killer.

Hand Position

Spanking requires some practice, especially if you have never hit something or someone before. For many women, it can be an eye-opener because we don't realize it can be trickier than it seems. One wrong slap could injure your fingers or your wrists. Keep the palm open with fingers together to begin. Hit a large area to begin and start light. Once your hand feels fine, then you can increase the intensity.

Types of Strikes

There are several ways to strike—short strokes or long, harder whacks. Always begin with short, light types with your hand then progress to longer, harder strokes and tools. Start with a short number interspersed with massaging. Shallow strikes on the surface of the skin can come from fast movements that burn and leave behind lines and welts. Once your man is able to handle short strikes, then you can slowly evolve to longer and harder whacks. Try to space out where you hit to allow the skin to recover.

Mix Up Striking with Other Sensations

Strikes can be mixed up with caressing, tickling, pinching, scratching or grabbing the butt. Try adding light strokes of running a paddle or a whip along the leg or lightly touching the feet and leading up to the genitals.

Rhythm

Feel free to mix up the rhythm. Do fast and slow strikes to change things. Check with your man by asking, "You like that?" If he likes it, switch it up. I have gone so far as to add mini spanking sessions during my sex sessions. I often use it to break up the monotony and keep things sexy and interesting. A couple of fast spanks gets us both in the mood, and my partner enjoys when I randomly rip off his pants and give him a spanking bent over the counter or furniture. Be aware of what works and what does not. Your man may prefer soft slaps, or they may be like the man covered in Saran Wrap who demands much harder whacks. Keep the rhythm even and the massage session directly after so that your man can look forward to a break. Don't give more than two or three long hard lashes before mixing it with short ones. You want your man to enjoy the session, but not hate it so much he will never want to do it again.

CHAPTER **17**

After Your Spanking Session

I t is important to have a light discussion about how the session went, what went well and what could have been omitted. Be honest and keep the conversation open and constructive. This is a great time for you both to learn how to improve the sessions. Feel free to add some treats, water, chocolate, tea, aloe vera, or muscle cream. Sometimes there may be an emotional release. Allow these things to happen naturally. The more open the discussion, the better your sessions. I have witnessed my partner hating spanking in the beginning, only to request it over and over later. Sometimes the discussions helped us to uncover what techniques were the best.

Things to Do

- Communicate before, during, and after.

- Practice with your tools beforehand on a pillow.

- Test your tools on yourself to learn their intensity.

- Choose a safety word.

- Watch body language.

- Deliver aftercare.

- Have a medical kit readily available.

Things Not to Do

- Begin too hard too fast.

- Hit too hard or frequently.

- Play if someone has bleeding disorders or is on medication that affects bleeding.

- Hit near the spine, kidneys, or other vital organs.

- Overdo it—permanent damage is a no-no.

How to Improve Communication

1. **Learn to be calm and relaxed.** If a conversation is making you angry, anxious, or frustrated, learning to self-soothe is key. If you respond from an angry place, or if you are anxious, nervous, or scared, you are likely to say words you don't mean, things that are hurtful, point blame, and/or criticize. Practice breathing. Take long deep breaths and count to ten. Go outside for some fresh air. It's okay to say, "I will be right back, I need a break." Practice breathing often, not just during a heated conversation, but while driving, while at your desk, even while relaxing. Breathing is at the core of becoming calm. And the absolute best time to talk is when you are calm.

2. **Be nonjudgmental.** Shut your critical and emotional mind off and really listen to what your partner is saying.

Empathize by putting yourself in your partner shoes, if you need to.

3. **Use positive language.** This is also about remembering to avoid blaming, pointing the finger, criticizing, and judging. Instead, reveal your feelings. For example, instead of saying, "You don't even try to please me," try this: "I really feel unsatisfied with our lovemaking these days." Focus on using "I feel" and avoid using "you" in the sentence.

4. **Listen.** Summarize, paraphrase, or repeat what your partner has said. This is an easy way to let your partner know you have heard them and can often diffuse an angry situation. If your partner says, "I am angry and sexually frustrated these days, and you don't seem to care about sex." Instead of responding defensively, which might be your inkling, this is a great opportunity for you to make the conversation productive. You can respond by saying, "It sounds like you are feeling dissatisfied with our sex life. Perhaps we could find a solution."

5. **Touch while talking.** Holding your partner's hand or putting your hand on his/her knee can remind you and your partner that you are on his/her side, and that you two are in this together. It promotes intimacy.

6. **Compliment.** Compliments are a big part of positive talk. It's essential for our partners to feel recognized and appreciated. I recommend a minimum of three compliments a day. The best way to catch a bee is with sugar.

Marisa Rudder

CHAPTER **18**

How to Spice Up Your Sex Life

Here are some great tips for spicing up your overall sex life:

1. **Have an affair with your partner**. Plan your date and pretend that you both are having an affair with each other. Seduce each other, tease, and be sexy and adventurous.

2. **Bed roles.** Dressing like another human is an easy way for all your secret desires to be achieved without an affair. Try to be a physician, a patient, a teacher, a student, or even a soldier.

3. **Think like a kid.** As a young teenager, you may have fallen in love. But that doesn't mean now and then you shouldn't behave like one. Make yourself creative and act like you're 18 years old on the weekend. Dress like one, hang out, and make yourself like teenagers.

4. **Focus on Foreplay.** The emphasis on foreplay is one of the best ways to have great sex. Only spend fifteen more minutes getting horny before having sex. You're both going to have better sex finally. During those fifteen minutes, caress and praise one another's body.

5. **Make sex unforeseen and unforeseeable.** No matter how complicated it might seem, avoid planning sex or programming sex unless you are both busy.

6. **Be innovative and shockingly fair.** As the relationship matures, new ways to become creative must be created. Treat yourself to something that makes your heart race and your sex life super sexy.

7. **Get your bed sexy stuff.** Bring your bed with fresh anticipation. Visit your nearest pharmacy or an adult shop and expose your senses to sex toys, lubricants, pheromones, and everything else.

8. **Feel sexy.** Look cute, and if you have to, continue to work out. Give yourself a sweet look, wear sexy lingerie, and get a new haircut for yourself. Feel sexy, and you're going to look sexy.

9. **Live the dreams of your wildest ones.** Just because you have a long-term relationship does not mean you shouldn't embrace your fantasies. Talk to your friend about it and enjoy it together.

10. **Practice withdrawal.** It'll lose its charm if you know you can have sex whenever you want. Stop having sex every now and then— and save it for days if you go clubbing or relax a bit. Plan this right, and it could be an enormous turn on.

11. **Shock factor.** Sexually shock one another. Surprise your partner occasionally into a sexual high. Surprise him when he comes home naked or tell him that when both of you come out to dinner, you're not wearing your panties under your short skirt.

12. **Think beyond the bed.** Think beyond the bed. In addition to the bed, there are many attractive areas. Think

of a kitchen, couch, toilet, patio, or swimming pool. Get creative, and it will be more fun to reward people.

13. **Add Food.** Fill the mood with food and drinks. Give meals or cook together. Aphrodisiac food will make your love more romantic and make you drink and horny with a few drinks.

14. **Massages with sensuality**. Get naked and give one another a sex-free sensual massage. Seek pleasure and encourage your fingers to linger for a while. As long as your partner's orgasm is focused on, it will make you both feel good.

15. **Try tantric Sex.** Bring tantric sex into the bedroom for an intense and passionate sexual encounter.

16. **Think kinky.** There is nothing to remove the thrill of wild sex when the relationship starts to slow down in bed. Discuss your dreams and give life to your fetishes and extravagant wishes.

17. **Take a fun vacation from time to time.** Choose a holiday destination that you both want, whether it's a crowded sex resort or a lovely idyllic paradise island. So, spend all your holidays just dreaming of sexy feelings.

18. **Calling and sending hot emails**. Don't wait until you seduce your partner. Just send a few sexy pictures in the middle of the day and taunt your partner if you both want to meet at night.

19. **Watch porn.** Sometimes watching porn helps both of you to get in the mood and make love better by watching a couple on the screen.

20. **Fool around**. Do not try to tie yourself up with each other for any time alone. Be loving to each other all the time and sometimes take affection to an entirely new level.

If they are on the phone, take their pants off and give them an oral call in the middle of a phone call.

21. **Body play**. Instead of having sex, play with each other's bodies. Paint with glow-in-the-dark or edible colors on your partner's body.

22. **Make a video from home.** Create a video while you have sex together. Delete it, if you make a sex tape or hide it in a secure place after the act has been done. Watching you age in the video and concurrently can be a massive rush for everyone.

23. **Wear revealing clothing.** Show something, and make it look like an accident, every now and then.

24. **Using mirrors.** Use full-length mirrors to increase your sexual experience alongside your bed. When you want to recreate a foursome romantic dream, you can have sex very close to the mirror. See or imagine a new pair of yourself.

25. **Make a little bit of noise.** Moaning or whispering sexy nothings in bed is an enormous turn on that cannot be explained. Speak in bed, and in no time, you're going to wake up your partner.

26. **Sexual configuration.** Give your room a glimpse of sex. Use perfumes and candles to make lovemaking feel like a luxurious luxury.

27. **Be real.** You cannot enjoy or even be faithful to the best sex in your life until you both share thoughts and sexual memories, whether it be about a romantic obsession or a sentimental memory, with each other. Don't be mentally awkward, and your sex relationship will flourish.

28. **Read an erotic novel together.** The spirit is our most significant sexual organ. Build and envision dreams. It's going to be a more substantial turn than you think.

29. **Creating sexual memory.** Always try something new. Having sex in a car or on a beach during a holiday, swimming nude in a pool, or even as a couple in bed. So as long as you both continuously make fresh and exciting memories, sex will never get boring.

30. **Be faithful to the relationship.** Notwithstanding love and trust in the air, nothing can tarnish your relationship than unfaithfulness. You may go so far as to swing or engage in other kinky ideas. But as long as there is love and confidence, you can find a way to rekindle the sexual excitement without getting lost. You will probably stand the test of time if you're just looking for opportunities to get better sex with your partner and not for a means to fool your partners.

Enjoy the bliss of romance and keep your passion boiling together with new and sexy things.

Marisa Rudder

CHAPTER **19**

Relationship Discipline

D iscipline is the practice in which the dominant, the Queen, sets rules that the submissive, the man, is expected to obey. When rules of expected behavior are broken, punishment is often used as a means of disciplining. Discipline is one of the foundations of BDSM, but today it has made its way into many other types of relationships, including Female Led Relationship where the Queen is in charge. In relationship discipline, rules can be made so that a submissive knows how they should behave and ensure the dominant is not displeased. Rules can also be for reminding subs of their inferior status, or for training a novice sub.

When such rules are broken, punishment is often used as a means of discipline. Punishment itself can be physical, such as spanking or psychological, such as public humiliation or a combination of both. The goal of discipline is to teach the sub that they have made a mistake so that they learn self-restraint and become a better sub in the future. The punishment is generally related to the mistake and is generally proportional to the severity and frequency of the mistake. Punishments done on the submissive is for disciplining, in response to violations of predetermined rules, or for otherwise displeasing the dominant. Punishment is considered necessary to change the behavior, as without it, a sub may repeat mistakes.

Discipline is not abuse. In a "fun" scenario, this could play out in a scene in which the submissive, your man, has been "naughty" and might deserve a spanking, paddling, etc. This is a type of role-play, given in mock punishment, for mutual enjoyment and entertainment. It is an act of mischievous play, a reward of pleasurable attention by engaging in an activity that is enjoyable to both. Contrast this to something that is more serious, real punishment is rarely enjoyable for either the submissive or the dominant. Punishment is a tool, used to adjust the submissive's behavior to a more desired state or outcome. It requires effort, attention, and often consumes time that could have been spent doing something fun or enjoyable. Instead of enjoyment, the participants are now working on something that probably could have been avoided. Definitely not fun.

The same occurs in a Female Led Relationship. The female is in charge, and she is the Queen. Many people confuse strong females in relationships with a dominatrix. The two are not related. A woman leading in her relationship is much different than being paid to hurt and punish someone. Even though in some relationships the Queen and her man may want to engage in some punishment or light BDSM, there is still a difference. The Female Led Relationship is all about females leading in marriages or long-term relationships.

Part of relationship discipline is the use of a contract. A contract is an easy and uniform way for a submissive and dominant—even people who have never met before—to establish protocol, boundaries and safety within a scene. Although it might seem silly or even like overkill to those who are new to relationship discipline and BDSM, using a contract can make it easier for you to exchange information that would prove an otherwise awkward conversation. A contract helps you and your man to decide on what is allowed and not allowed in the relationship and what the consequences are for breaking the contract. It may also include establishing a safe word and clearly defining what you both want.

Some examples include the Queen to be addressed as 'My Queen' or the Sub will do the dishes every night or make the bed. During sex, everything will be allowed except anal sex or no more than ten lashes during spanking. A light contract can be used to ensure both of you adhere to the rules. I can recall walking into my friend's study and seeing a board up on the wall with her and her husband's name. Written under the names were their respective duties that were ticked off each day. In essence, my friend had created a type of contract that clearly outlined what was expected.

A light contract can be as follows:

Chosen safe word:

Name/title of Queen:

Name/title of the man during scene:

Are there any other concerns? List here.

What Are the Duties:

What is the Punishment:

Any other concerns:

Man Signature_____

Queen Signature_____

A more serious contract can be as follows:

I, YOUR MAN, request of QUEEN, the acceptance of my submission. I grant ownership of my mind and body and accept your care and protection of free will and open heart. Through this agreement, we may strengthen our bond and increase intimacy.

I vow to provide my body to fulfill your every need. Use of my body will be at your discretion. Furthermore, I will strive to better serve your needs and accept your guidance along this journey.

To this end, I will adapt my physical, emotional and mental attitudes to the best of my ability.

I trust that you will provide guidance during sex and daily that helps me grow as a submissive and during life to spur my growth as a person.

Whether together or separated, I surrender control of my sexual pleasure and physical and emotional comfort to you. Additionally, I agree that no secrets shall exist between us, and all questions will be answered honestly, and privacy must be granted to me by the Queen. It is therefore my responsibility to voice all fantasies, limits, feelings and needs without hesitance to you and to work to eliminate mental hurdles that may prevent such communication.

I accept any punishment that you see fit should I fail to uphold this contract and not meet your expectations.

I grant you ownership of my mind, body and soul with the understanding that my physical, emotional and mental safety will be cared for. Risk of life or livelihood allows for termination of this contract.

Should the need to revise the contract arise before the expiration date, I agree to verbal negotiation.

The consent in this contract begins on [Date]. This contract will expire in [# Days/Weeks/Months], at which point, the contract may be renewed, or a new contract may be created and agreed upon.

MAN Signature_____

QUEEN Signature_____

Relationship discipline can use positive reinforcement, a reward system or punishment. Some couples enjoy discipline with the use of punishments in the following forms:

- Wear chastity belts.

- Denial of orgasm.

- Early bedtime.

- Go without food for a day.

- Deny orgasms for x number of days or weeks or months.

- Take away the right to publicly speak for themselves for x number of –hours.

- Deny them attention or the right to come over and see you.

- If there is more than one slave, make them prepare you to have sex with your other slaves. They get nothing and must watch.

- Take away anything they enjoy or love for x number of days, etc.

- If they don't like collars, make them wear one around the house. If they love their collar, take it away.

- X number of lashes of spanking while standing.

- Standing in a corner for x number hours.

Punishments can take the form of errands or daily chores:

- Run an errand wearing a long coat with nothing underneath.

- Get the groceries.

- Do their daily routine around the house naked.

- Serve breakfast in bed for a week.

- Bow every time he greets you.

- Allow you to watch any show you want for a month.

Punishments in the form of sex:

- Give the Queen only oral sex for a week.

- Massage the Queen's body for a week.

- Surprise you with something sexy each week for a month.

- Orgasm denial for a week and wearing his chastity belt.

- Get spanked each night for a week with a different tool.

Relationship discipline involves three specific parts:

- Correction – taking time out to discuss the delay in assignment, the nature of the challenge/resistance, how to get past it, setting a new deadline & expectations. This requires clear communication and investment of time so that you are setting the submissive for success. Correction has three main parts (1) building Awareness, (2) providing Education, (3) framing the consequence or outcome.

- Discipline – discipline focuses on a challenging task that will build or focus on a new skill for development. May include areas such as developing self-control, personal accountability, better communication, deeper understanding, etc. These usually come in form of an exercise, drills, or a challenge that is actively watched and coached by the dominant partner. It may also be removal of a privilege that is providing a distraction. Discipline builds on a prior correction (which is a necessary component) and adds to it with practical and focused effort.

- Punishment – it is often a punitive experience that is the consequence for failing to execute or obey. Ideally, however, a punishment given is meant to override the cognitive mind and speak to the subconscious or primal mind directly, usually by associating the negative behavior/action with a negative consequence. These consequences often take the form of removal of unrelated privileges, denials of requests, subjection to discomfort, pain, humiliation, etc. This is the price or cost of disobedience, stubbornness, etc.

- Punishment as an ordeal – Punishment also serves as a physical start and end to a problem. When used as an ordeal, the punishment is given to allow the subject to move on without carrying mental or emotional burden. Some subs or slaves will carry a mistake with them, invisibly beating themselves up. Others will expect a harsh punishment, and if not given, will constantly anticipate it "at any time," By using punishment as an ordeal, it can create a firm and tangible break between what happened Before and After. This allows the sub to leave the past in the past and move forward knowing punishment is done and over with.

Both the Queen and her man must decide on what the punishments will be. Many people will frown upon the use of these tactics, but relationship discipline has transformed relationships because both people are 100 percent present. Let's face it—sexual fantasy and desire are another reason why a Queen and her male subject will sometimes add discipline and spanking into their relationship. Often the man and his Queen may view the disciplinary process as merely a prelude to sex or part of sex. If a couple views discipline as a form of foreplay, then it is easy to gloss over the disciplinary aspect of spanking in one's hurry to get to the sexual side of matters. Although this may fulfill an immediate desire for sexual connection and release, it certainly creates a lot of frustration and resentment in the man, which will return later in the form of disobedience and juvenile behavior. A Queen needs to exert the control when it comes to discipline before sex.

As part of the Female Led Relationship, the Queen needs to do the discipline. He focuses on her sexual fulfillment. The Queen is in charge, so she can properly discipline her male subject and then require him to perform oral sex on her until satisfied. This is a simple matter of priorities, but it doesn't mean that it is easy. It can be quite difficult to separate relationship discipline and sexual discipline as foreplay, but each Queen should keep it mind.

If a Queen feels her desire for sex is so strong that she cannot discipline her man properly first, then she can resolve the problem differently. She can discipline him after they have had sex. This may sound a little unusual to some people, but it is the perfect solution for many Queens. If discipline makes a woman think of sex more than of punishment, the simplest solution is to go ahead and make love first. After the lovemaking has come to its natural conclusion, disciplining her man for his misbehavior can replace cuddling. As long as she isn't so exhausted by her orgasms that she has no more energy, there is no reason why the Queen can't discipline her man after lovemaking, as well as, before.

Marisa Rudder

CHAPTER **20**

Spanking to Relieve Stress

A s mentioned previously, spanking can be very therapeutic to both the Queen doing the act and the man. Sometimes spanking has been used for therapy, but it is only done so by a qualified therapist. However, it is possible to utilize some of the basic techniques to conduct spanking sessions aimed at relieving stress. Begin with consent from both the Queen and her man. Men who desire spanking from their Queen can actually benefit from a spanking session aimed at relieving stress. The following is a type of spanking session that may be used for the purpose of helping your man to release unwanted stress.

The Process:

1. Both the Queen and her man need to have clear expectations of the need for and the desired results of therapeutic spanking.

2. Choose a ritual that works for both partners and follow without deviation once established.

3. Use a timer for a standard 30-minute session that involves both spanking and talking designed to help, not hurt.

4. Set a clear date and time for the session that must be adhered to.

5. Choose a location away from distractions.

The Session:

1. The Queen and her man must treat the appointment seriously, and the Queen should role-play rather than be the normal partner.

2. The man must be fully prepared and committed.

3. Add some dress up.

4. Start promptly.

Preparation:

1. Get all tools ready.

2. Choose a warm inviting sexy space.

3. Put away all phones and lock the door to prevent intrusions from pets or kids.

4. The Queen must give all orders.

5. Invite your man to remove clothing below the waist and lay over the spanker's lap.

6. On the floor at your man's head should be a box of tissues and the timer already running.

The Spanking:

1. Begin the spanking by repeating the reasons for the session.

2. After the man finishes speaking, the Queen should begin with a shorthand spanking.

3. Again, the goal is not to punish but to utilize spanking to mentally break free of whatever is stressing the man.

4. The Queen should always use leading questions such as: What is causing your stress? What changes can you make? Why does this make you so unhappy?

5. The Queen needs to pay close attention and spank harder as needed if progress is not being made in answering.

6. Listen to your man's answers.

7. Repeat the leading questions and allow time for him to answer.

8. Add some intensity slowly.

9. Keep the flow of feedback going by asking how he is feeling.

10. The goal is always to allow your man to concentrate on stress reduction.

11. Allow your man to show any emotional response that he needs to let out.

After Care:

1. When the timer goes off, the spanking is over.

2. Your man should remain in position for at least an additional five minutes.

3. The Queen should massage and apply lotion to the spanked areas. No sexual contact until your man has rest.

4. Hug him and make him feel loved.

CHAPTER **21**

What is Transformational Discipline?

When it is necessary to transform your partner and get more serious about spanking, then you can use a Transformational Discipline. Transformational Discipline goes beyond a normal spanking and transforms the man. It is a spanking that creates some kind of quantum leap in his behavior, his attitude and his understanding. It is a discipline that gives him a total emotional, spiritual and moral makeover. There must be consent from him before you both decide to engage in this as it can bring about some deep changes.

A Transformational Discipline is intended to create genuine submission in the disciplined men. This is not the kind of submission that involves the man submitting only when it suits him to submit. This is the kind of submission that is lasting and genuine. A Transformational Discipline is also meant to teach him true obedience. Most couples enjoy this level of discipline with spanking, but the man generally will feel he needs it to completely submit to a woman in a Female Led Relationship. I have personally had many requests for this, but it is reserved for serious sessions.

A Transformational Discipline can be painful. This pain may consist primarily of physical pain. The spanking that a man receives may be harsher and more severe than a normal punishment. On the other hand, a Transformational Discipline may also be painful because of its emotional content—due to the emotional experiences that the man has during his punishment. The physical spanking may not be any harsher than a normal punishment spanking, but the emotional effects of the discipline on the punished man may be deeper and longer lasting.

The need for Transformational Discipline arises when a man needs to be disciplined in a way that creates a significant change in his behavior and attitude, beyond what he normally experiences as a result of a regular punishment spanking. A Transformational Discipline becomes necessary when the Queen recognizes her man's need for a proper spanking that transforms his mind and heart. She is seeking to teach him to become more positive and healthier in his outlook and comportment than he currently is. A man's misbehavior may be due to more than one cause. That is why often a single spanking will not be enough to cure a particular problem that the man has with his behavior or attitude. He may be disciplined one week for misbehavior and then must be punished again the following week for the same kind of disobedience, disrespect or dishonesty.

It does not mean that he didn't learn her lesson from the first spanking. It simply means that the first spanking dealt with one aspect of his negativity in feelings or thoughts, which uncovered another problem that lay beneath. It has been previously explained that dealing with a man's repeated negative behavior or attitude is often like peeling an onion— the cause of his problem may be multi-layered. This multi-causal nature of some examples of feminine misbehavior is why it is often necessary to spank a woman for the same misbehavior on more than a single occasion.

Transformational Discipline is not necessarily designed to overcome this problem of the multi-layered causes of the man's misbehavior. It may work in this way, but it is not specifically intended to do so. The Queen must not attempt to accelerate his learning process too much by administering a Transformational Discipline just because she wants to speed things up.

The Queen will often get better results if she concentrates on giving one spanking at a time. Giving him a major session all at once in which he is unable to sit down for weeks will not work and can make the man unwilling to participate. If the Queen feels she has given him enough time to modify his behavior and attitude to be more positive, yet still he still has not made the changes that she wants, then she is justified in administering a Transformational Discipline. The Queen must be patient with her man. If he does not make an effort to modify his behavior and attitude to more positive ways, she can use a Transformational Discipline. This will teach a man the true meaning of submission. He will learn not only to submit to her punishment but also to submit to his Queen.

The man in need of a Transformational Discipline will also usually have a strong need to be taught better obedience. The Transformational Discipline he receives will teach him obedience in a thorough and uncompromising way. He will learn to be more obedient to the Queen so that he has fewer problems of misbehavior in the future. He will learn obedience and especially the disciplinary process that his Queen initiates for his benefit.

A Queen needs to be consistent when she punishes her man for bad behavior. This means that she needs to ensure he is always punished for any disciplinable offense that he may

Marisa Rudder

commit. It means that he is always punished for bad behavior. If he breaks a rule or behaves in any manner that is quite obviously dishonest, disrespectful or disobedient to the Queen, then it follows that he should be disciplined for this masculine bad behavior. He must be punished.

Inconsistent punishment is when a man is allowed to get away with bad behavior. He may sometimes be disciplined for unruly behavior but at other times, identical negative behavior or attitude may pass totally unpunished. This inconsistency will surprise the man. It may relieve the man if he has been afraid of being punished for his bad behavior. But the truth is, inconsistent punishment will disappoint and frustrate a man. One of the primary causes of increased masculine disobedience to his Queen is inconsistent punishment of his bad behavior. It is vital that the Queen always punish her man when he misbehaves. It is critical for his development as an obedient man that she does so.

If a man misbehaves, punishment must be automatic and swift. I found the best results occur when the man has to say what he is getting the spanking for. What is the transgression and what did he do to deserve the spanking? The Queen is free to use her lap, a counter or standing to administer the spanking. It is worth noting that consistent punishment does not always mean immediate punishment. Some men incorrectly imagine immediacy equals consistency, and sometimes it can be much more productive for the Queen to inform him that his misbehavior will be dealt with later that day. This leaves the man with the awareness that he is going to be disciplined for his bad behavior, and even thinking about his discipline will improve his behavior. That's why a delayed punishment can have a better effect than an immediate punishment because the man has a lot of time to reflect on the spanking or whipping he is going to receive, as well as having a lot of time to reflect on what he did to deserve his upcoming spanking or whipping. Many men prefer to get their punishment over and done with because they realize the waiting period before the spanking is an additional discipline in itself.

What is Upkeep Discipline?

Upkeep Discipline is one of the most important techniques used in the female led lifestyle. Upkeep Discipline has an incredible number of benefits for the man and for the couple. Among other things, Upkeep Discipline will act as a regular and frequent reminder to the man that he is subject to discipline by his Queen for his bad behavior. It will help to maintain his good behavior and good attitude. It will reduce the need for many punishment spankings since his behavior will tend to be better as a result of the Queen's Upkeep Discipline session. The key to Upkeep Discipline is a regular schedule. The typical and recommended interval for Upkeep Discipline is once a week, but some Queen's find that they need to use Upkeep Discipline every two or three days, or even daily. If a Queen has been giving her man a weekly Upkeep Discipline, it is normally important to keep that regular schedule in place to maintain consistency. If a scheduled Upkeep Discipline is missed, the woman's behavior and attitude will generally suffer, because the Queen's consistency has been damaged.

Since the key to Upkeep Discipline is regularity, anything that reduces or eliminates regularity is going to adversely affect the man and his behavior. It is critical to ensure that Upkeep Discipline is given regularly to men. When the Queen takes charge and makes really good, well-thought-out decisions, it's pretty easy for men to submit. Why not? The woman has made the right call and all he has to do is go along with her. A man needs consistency from his Queen because he needs to feel loved. When his Queen is inconsistent with any aspect of her practice of female led discipline, the man will begin to feel unloved. This is usually a complete misunderstanding of his Queen's motives, of course, but according to the rules of masculine logic, his Queen doesn't love him if she fails to discipline him consistently.

It is important for his Queen to realize this and to make the connection between disciplining her man and his perception of whether she loves him or not. Giving him consistent discipline is giving him attention, which is a simple and effective way to remind him that the Queen is in charge and does love him. It shows she cares enough to discipline him for his bad behavior. A Queen who doesn't care at all about her man will simply let her do whatever he wants because she feels completely separate from him. She does not feel as though she has a shared destiny with him. But a Queen who cares for a man will discipline him for his own good since she wants what is best for him, even if she must bring him to tears in the process.

Being in a Female Led Relationship where the Queen is consistent gives a great feeling of emotional security to a man. The moral courage and strength that his Queen displays every time he is disciplined for bad behavior is a sign that she is strong enough to lead him. And as you know, a man's worst enemy is himself. When a Queen has been loving and kind enough to provide him with the deep emotional security that comes from living the female led lifestyle, she needs to be aware of what she has given him. If she suddenly becomes inconsistent with her discipline, he will feel the painful loss of this emotional security. He will feel lost and lonely. He will feel as though he exposed his innermost need for discipline to her, but that she has retreated from her promise to stand firm against his bad masculine behavior. Additionally, she has retreated from her promise to punish him whenever he misbehaves.

Consistent discipline is also important because it reduces or eliminates the man's juvenile behavior. A man behaves like a juvenile when he feels that his Queen is not really committed to the female led lifestyle, or when he wants to test her resolve, or for other different reasons. But consistency is an important part of preventing juvenile behavior because the man is taught at all times that he is responsible for his actions and words, and that any misbehavior will be consistently punished by his Queen with spanking or even more harsh discipline. There is no need for this kind of childish male behavior. It is a form of testing, and if his Queen consistently disciplines him for bad behavior, it will remove any doubt in the man's mind. However, a lack of consistency is not an excuse for juvenile male behavior. It may be a contributing factor in juvenile behavior, but it is not an excuse for such misconduct.

One of the most important reasons for consistency is that it simply reduces all forms of bad masculine behavior. A consistent approach to discipline will reduce disobedience. It sounds rather obvious but is worth restating because many men are quite indignant about their Queen's apparent lack of consistency. Sometimes a man can focus more on the inconsistency of his Queen rather than his own masculine misbehavior that arises as a result of it. But misbehavior is the most severe consequence of inconsistent approaches to a female led discipline of a man in which the primary goal of the punishment is to deal with male misbehavior. It has other benefits, but that is the single most important one. A lack of consistency will result in a higher incidence of masculine disobedience, disrespect and dishonesty.

As one might also expect, a lack of consistency also results in significantly greater disharmony in the Female Led

Relationship. A firm and reassuring framework of female led discipline provides help for a man who is lost or damaged. Consistency is optimal. Male misbehavior tends to tear and attack the harmony and peace between the man and his woman found in a loving Female Led Relationship. While it is the man's misbehavior that causes this negative impact, it is also the Queen's lack of consistency that has allowed the bad masculine behavior to surface.

Conclusion

Spanking is a wonderful way to add some spice to your sex life and your relationship. Spanking has its origins in BDSM, but whether you prefer to keep things light and fun, or use spanking along with a more serious form of relationship discipline, this will be decided by you and your Queen. Spanking works perfectly with Female Led Relationships where the Queen is naturally in-charge and the man is the supportive gentleman and sub. While *Love & Obey* does not support abuse or non-consensual punishment, we support the idea of spanking for fun and discipline with consent.

Couples are encouraged to get creative with tools, costumes, roles and spanking positions. The perfect spanking session must begin with communication, warm up and preparation. Spanking may be used as foreplay or as mini stand-alone sessions. The power dynamic explored between the Queen and her man can be very exciting. Spanking shows no signs of slowing down. It still has searches in the hundreds of thousands, and it has become one of the favorite pastimes of more than 60 percent of couples. Spanking has the power to transform a relationship. The goal is always happy, safe spanking.

Marisa Rudder